Kingston Libraries

THE ROYAL BOROUGH OF
**KINGSTON**
UPON THAMES

## On line Services

# www.kingston.gov.uk/libraries

Renew a book (5 times)     Request a book
Change of address     Email a branch
Library news and updates     Get your pin
Search the catalogues     s free reference sites

**020 85** ‖‖‖‖‖‖ **006**

| | 0 3 APR 20... | |
|---|---|---|
| 1/20 | | |
| | | |
| | | |
| | | |
| | | |

# DOCTOR WHO

# THE DALEK HANDBOOK
## Steve Tribe and James Goss

**BBC**
BOOKS

1 3 5 7 9 10 8 6 4 2

Published in 2011 by BBC Books,
an imprint of Ebury Publishing.
A Random House Group Company

Doctor Who is a BBC Wales production for
BBC One. Executive producers: Steven Moffat,
Piers Wenger and Beth Willis

The Random House Group Limited
Reg. No. 954009

Addresses for companies within the
Random House Group can be found at
www.randomhouse.co.uk

A CIP catalogue record for this book is
available from the British Library.

ISBN 978 1 849 90232 8

The Random House Group Limited supports the
Forest Stewardship Council (FSC), the leading
international forest certification organisation.
All our titles that are printed on Greenpeace
approved FSC certified paper carry the FSC logo.
Our paper procurement policy can be found at
www.randomhouse.co.uk/environment

*For Lucy, Kieran and Jacob*

Commissioning editor: **Albert DePetrillo**
Creative consultant: **Justin Richards**
Editorial manager: **Nicholas Payne**
Project editor: **Kari Speers**
Designer: **Paul Lang**
Production: **Phil Spencer**

Printed and bound in Germany by
Firmengruppe APPL, aprinta druck, Wemding

To buy books by your favourite authors
and register for offers, visit
**www.randomhouse.co.uk**

BBC Books would like to thank the following
for providing photographs and for permission
to reproduce copyright material. While every
effort has been made to trace and acknowledge
all copyright holders, we would like to apologise
should there have been any errors or omissions.
All images copyright © BBC, except:
Page 5 courtesy Kit Bevan; page 24
courtesy Andrew Beech; page 31 © Express
Newspapers; pages 47 (bottom), 54 (top), 68
(top left), 76 (bottom left), 93 and 140 (top
right) courtesy *Doctor Who Magazine*; page
54 (bottom) courtesy *Radio Times*; page 87
(right) courtesy David Richardson; pages
90–2 design drawings courtesy Universal
Television; pages 96–8 courtesy Big Finish
Productions; page 99 (bottom right) courtesy
Telos Publishing Limited; page 109 concept
art by Matt Savage, courtesy the *Doctor Who*
Art Department; pages 134–5 and 152–5
concept art by Peter McKinstry, courtesy the
*Doctor Who* Art Department; page 140
(bottom left) courtesy G.E. Fabbri Ltd.
Page 1 illustration by Lee Johnson;
page 27 (bottom) illustration by Peter Archer
from *Doctor Who and the Daleks* by
David Whitaker (1965 edn.); pages 150–1
illustrations by Gavin Rymill

With additional thanks to: **Richard Bignell,
Lee Binding, Nicholas Briggs, Antoinette Burchill,
Raymond P. Cusick, Russell T Davies, Mark Gatiss,
Leanne Gill, Ed Griffiths, Ian Grutchfield, Dan Hall,
David J. Howe, Richard Martin, Steve Maher, Peter
McKinstry, Steven Moffat, Glenn Ogden, Helen Raynor,
Edward Russell, Gary Russell, Matt Savage, Robert
Shearman, Oli Smith, Tom Spilsbury, Ed Stradling,
Lee Sullivan, Mike Tucker, David Turbitt and Peter Ware.**

# CONTENTS

# INTRODUCTION

D aleks! The Doctor's deadliest enemies, but also his earliest champions. If it hadn't been for the Daleks, there might be no *Doctor Who* today – the show would probably be just a footnote in television history, an ambitious but long-forgotten teatime drama.

But because writer Terry Nation had the brilliant idea of a race of deadly mutants, because producer Verity Lambert defied her bosses and insisted his script got made, and because designer Raymond Cusick came up with that amazing, timeless blueprint, *Doctor Who* was transformed from a moderate success into a hit. Nation knew how to hook viewers, and the audience nearly doubled as the show's second serial went on, breaking the 10 million mark and taking *Doctor Who* into TV's weekly top 30.

That audience refused to let the Daleks die. As parents, teachers and newspapers started to notice children imitating Daleks in school playgrounds, the programme makers realised they'd have to bring the Daleks back. Before long, the Daleks were invading not just 22nd-century Earth but also 1960s toyshops and cinemas. Since then, the Daleks have faced every Doctor, returning in more stories than any other monster. They have been voted a British design icon.

They've graced postage stamps. They've advertised chocolate bars. And they've helped *Doctor Who* return in its most successful incarnation yet – in 2008, Davros and a few million Daleks even helped make the show the most watched programme on television, for the first time in its history.

After almost fifty years, the Daleks remain incredibly popular, whether luring the Doctor to Churchill's London or imprisoning him in the Pandorica. *The Dalek Handbook* is a celebration of their success and a comprehensive guide to their history, from petrified jungle to fossilised Daleks.

The journey starts on the planet Skaro, where one man has come up with a terrible solution to an unending war.

'Now we can begin..'

# SKARO

The Daleks' original home is the planet Skaro, a world with a history of constant warfare. It is an inhospitable place: its atmosphere, while breathable, has been soaked with fluctuating levels of radiation for millennia, and its flora and fauna have suffered extensive mutation and are generally lethal. Few visitors to Skaro have escaped with their lives, so information is scarce, and the histories of its own inhabitants are at best unreliable. Its two dominant species have fought ceaseless wars with each other. The planet has been abandoned, destroyed and resurrected at least once. Some claim that Skaro is now a dead and empty world; others say that a great city has been rebuilt amidst its ruins. Have the Daleks returned to their ancestral home?

Skaro is the twelfth planet from its sun, and the only one in its solar system capable of supporting intelligent life. It has a faint system of rings encircling it, dominated by toxic gases, dust and debris from constant warfare on the planet's surface. Listed in some star charts as D5-Gamma-Z-Alpha, it has a reddish appearance and two known moons.

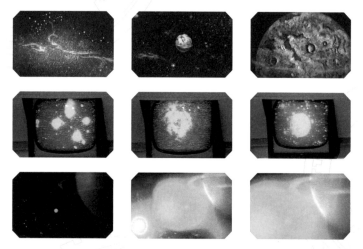

The planet's surface has been ravaged by conflict throughout its history. The dominant species were the Thals and the Kaleds, who fought a war that lasted a thousand years. It devastated the landscape, the atmosphere and the ecology, making Skaro one of the most inhospitable worlds in its galaxy. Yet life persisted.

Skaro's largest single landmass – named Dalazar in some accounts – covers one-third of the planet's surface and is divided by an enormous mountain range, creating twin continents. To the east of these Drammankin Mountains lie vast lakes bordering one of Skaro's least inhospitable regions. Here, between the lakes and an extensive jungle, is where first the Kaleds and later the Daleks built their cities; their bitter enemies, the Thals, had their own city surprisingly near to this site, and the uninhabited areas between the two could be traversed in a matter of hours.

The surrounding jungle and desert give way to slightly more habitable plateaux, where it was possible for a time to grow crops. Rainfall occurred only every four or five years, however, and the atmospheric changes wrought by the wars eventually put a stop even to that. By the 20th century (in Earth's timescale), Skaro was an arid wasteland, its lakes and caverns haunted by omnivorous mutations, its jungles petrified in a neutronic war, its soil turned to lifeless sand and ash.

Little could survive in those conditions…

# IMAGINING AN ICON

From June 1962, a weekly science-fiction series called *Out of this World* was broadcast on independent television. Three of its thirteen episodes were scripted by Terry Nation, until then a writer of radio comedies and the occasional movie screenplay, such as *What a Whopper!* (in which Adam Faith fakes the Loch Ness Monster). Meanwhile, BBC Television began work on its own new sci-fi series for a Saturday teatime slot, under the guidance of Sydney Newman and Donald Wilson, the Heads of Drama and Serials. They appointed David Whitaker as *Doctor Who*'s story editor, whose first task was to recruit writers. Nation was on Whitaker's list thanks to his work on *Out of this World*, but was already busy with scripts for comedian Tony Hancock, who advised him to reject the BBC's approach. When, soon after, Nation and Hancock fell out, the writer found himself unemployed and quickly wrote a pitch for Whitaker –

'The Survivors', in which the Daleks and Thals were joint victims of an alien neutron bomb attack.

On 31 July 1963, Whitaker formally commissioned a story from Nation under the title 'The Mutants'. As Nation developed his scripts, he dropped the alien aggressors and made the Daleks the villains of the piece. 'The Mutants' was intended to be the fourth or fifth story of *Doctor Who*'s run, following the accidental miniaturisation of the TARDIS travellers, their escape from the Stone Age, their encounter with a race of robots, and their journey to Cathay with Marco Polo. When two of these stories were dropped or postponed, Nation's storyline was moved and became *Doctor Who*'s second serial, *The Daleks*.

The new series was intended to be as educational as it was entertaining, using time travel as a means to explore scientific ideas and famous moments in history. So, when producer Verity Lambert presented Nation's scripts to Newman and Wilson, the Daleks were not a hit: 'Sydney wasn't very pleased about the Daleks. He came up to me and said, "I told you – no BEMs," which stood for Bug-Eyed Monsters.' The first serial had been made but 'there was a real wobble going round the BBC, and it was crucial that whatever we did next was a success. We didn't have a lot of choice – we only had the Dalek serial ready to go. David and I actually thought it was very good – exciting, and all the things that I would watch – but Donald hated it, too. We had a bit of a crisis of confidence, because Donald was so adamant that we shouldn't make it. Had we had *anything else* ready, we would have made that. Then, when we started doing it, it just seemed right.'

# FLORA AND FAUNA

The molecular basis of all organic life on Skaro is fundamental DNA type 989. Conditions on Skaro after millennia of warfare were so extreme that few of its indigenous life forms survived, fewer survived in anything like their original evolved forms, and some were not even organic...

## Mutos

From the first century of the thousand-year war, both sides deployed chemical weapons that wrought long-term physiological havoc on their victims. Huge numbers of Kaleds and Thals became grotesquely mutated, and that mutation passed into the planet's gene pool, creating a third distinct species of deformed humanoids. They were labelled 'Mutos', banished from the cities and condemned to scavenge in Skaro's wastelands. Though they were seen as an animal sub-species, they retained not only a strong survival instinct but also a keen awareness of morality and beauty, ironically lost by their warring 'superiors'.

## Animal Mutations

When Kaled research turned to genetic adaptation as the war approached its climax, there were countless failed experiments – animals whose evolution had been accelerated, reversed or tampered with to produce ghastly parodies of their original forms. Like the Mutos, these were discarded, left to rot outside the domes, but many of them thrived as outsized predators. Giant clam-like creatures, for example, lay in wait in the mountain caverns, the serrated edges of their shells able to take a man's leg off.

Some of these creatures infested the waters beyond the Drammankin Mountains, dominating what became known as the Lake of Mutations. The Lake was so badly irradiated its waters actually glowed, and the hideous creatures that lived in it bred and cross-bred, eventually providing a perfect natural defence for one side of the Dalek city.

# Slyther

The rate of mutation in Skaro's animal life was accelerated by the detonation of a neutron bomb; those creatures that survived the explosion became even more vicious and deadly. The Daleks eventually emerged from their city and reclaimed Skaro, capturing some of these monsters, among them the Slyther. Perfecting interstellar travel and beginning their assault on the galaxy, the Daleks would sometimes unleash Slythers on conquered planets. One was used as a semi-trained guard dog at the Daleks' primary mining operation in England, following their invasion of Earth.

# Magneton

Whether a creature made of metal could evolve naturally is unknown, but it is more likely that the Magneton was the descendent of some early experimental cyborg. A squat reptilian, not unlike a small crocodile, it had sharp spikes along its spine and eyes on extended stalks.

They were held together by an inner magnetic field, which also attracted their prey towards them, and their inert bodies could be used as an energy source.

# Varga Plants

The neutronic explosion left most plant life petrified, but radiation levels gradually decreased and some of Skaro's eco-system revived. Much of the vegetation, however, had also been radically affected by irradiation and experimentation. An extreme example was the Varga plant – taller than a man, it was actually mobile, using its roots to drag itself along the ground. It was covered in extremely sharp spines, with which it attacked all nearby animal life. But victims pierced by Varga thorns did not die – instead its infection rapidly transformed them into more Varga plants. Like the Slythers, the Vargas were exported from Skaro by the Daleks, and unleashed on other worlds, such as Kembel.

# DOMINANT SPECIES

The history of Skaro tells of two great races, locked in an unending war, which gave birth to the deadliest creatures in the universe...

## Kaleds

The Kaleds were a bipedal humanoid race, only distinguishable from their bitter enemies the Thals by their dark hair, suggesting a shared ancestry at some point in their prehistory. Both races resembled Earth's humans, although their blood and chemical make-up, encephalographic patterns and physiological composition were entirely different. They produced brilliant thinkers and scientists, most notably Davros, but their extreme self-belief and xenophobia led them into the long war against the Thals. They would be satisfied with nothing less than the total extermination of the Thals, and were prepared to condemn themselves to decades, perhaps centuries, of underground existence, forsaking daylight and fresh air for ceaseless weapons research. Like the Thals, they constructed a vast protective dome over their city, from which only their frontline troops ever emerged.

## Dals

Skaro was home to other evolved, intelligent species at one time. The Dals were teachers and philosophers against whom the warrior Thals fought a great war. They ultimately became extinct, either subsumed into the Kaled race or just obliterated by the Thals, whose later legends conflated the Dals with the Daleks.

## Thals

Whatever common heritage the Kaleds and Thals might once have shared, a thousand years of war left them entirely separated – geographically, politically and even physically. The Thals were a race of tall, blond humanoids. For centuries they were aggressive and militaristic and may well have initiated the thousand-year war. By its end, their city had been destroyed and they were all but wiped out. Some did survive, and fought on.

The long-term genetic damage already affecting both species was accelerated when the Daleks exploded a neutron bomb. The extreme mutation that took hold of the Thals progressed incredibly rapidly – after just 500 years it had come full circle and the Thals were once again tall, blond humanoids with no obvious physical defects. More than that, they had evolved philosophically, too, becoming instinctive pacifists. Their agrarian

civilisation was now fairly primitive, although they maintained supplies of drugs designed to ward off the radioactivity in the air. They settled on a plateau that was just about capable of agricultural exploitation, and became farmers. They were determined to avoid any future conflict, all but forgetting how to fight. The failure of their crops eventually forced them to move on, scouring Skaro for other sources of food and water, and this brought them into conflict once again with the Daleks.

Future generations would remain true to their pacifist beliefs, but were increasingly forced to fight on against the Daleks, simply to stay alive. By the 26th century, the Daleks had all but abandoned Skaro in pursuit of universal supremacy, and the Thals were taking the fight to them. It's a fight they eventually lost – by the 46th century, Skaro seemed uninhabited. The Thals had either been driven from their home world or, finally, wiped out entirely.

## Thal History

The Thals preserved a record of their 'history' on metallic slates in a large canister, although this was an incomplete simplification of events, told largely in pictograms. While it confused the Daleks and Kaleds with the Dals, it also contained star charts of the seven galaxies visible from Skaro, an indication of how much more advanced the planet's civilisations had been before their long war of attrition. Later Thal histories focused on the Doctor's arrival on their world and the subsequent 'Dalek War'; after a few centuries, these stories were widely assumed to be myths, and most Thals thought of Earth, humans and the TARDIS as mere fictions.

# FASCISM

We must keep the Kaled race pure.

The Daleks had their origins in Nazi Germany. The Second World War was a recent memory for most people in 1963, and the Dalek race would have seemed eerily familiar – a military machine convinced of its own racial superiority, with an unthinking intolerance for anything unlike it. 'People do now associate them with the Hitler salute, the arm going up and "Exterminate! Exterminate!"' explains Carole Ann Ford, who played the Doctor's granddaughter, Susan. 'They were totally inhuman and therefore there was no reasoning with them, no point of contact... You just couldn't imagine what they were thinking.'

There are many echoes of the Nazis in the story of the Daleks. Their mantra of obedience, their military might and their forced labour were all chilling echoes of the war. Even their famous battle cry had its roots in the Extermination Camps (*Vernichtungslager*) to which the Nazis despatched Jews, Gypsies, homosexuals, dissenters and the 'genetically inferior'.

These links were made more obvious in *Genesis of the Daleks* (1975), which depicted the Kaleds as a fascist state of black-clad soldiers, obsessed with ethnic cleansing, who regularly clicked their heels as they denounced each other. Davros's aide, Nyder, was creepily reminiscent of Himmler, founder of the SS, even down to the swept-over hair and wire-framed glasses. Actor Peter Miles's costume initially included a version of a German medal, the Iron Cross, although this was removed after a couple of episodes, when the production team decided it made the connection too explicit.

Terry Nation was not without a sense of irony. The Daleks' first enemy was the Thal race – Aryan giants, whose blond-haired, blue-eyed physical perfection embodied the Nazi ideal. The Daleks, by contrast, were a master race of terribly deformed mutants, incapable of surviving outside their casings and unable to breathe anything other than an atmosphere polluted by millennia of warfare.

# IF THEY CALL US MUTATIONS, WHAT MUST THEY BE LIKE?

The war between the Thals and the Kaleds raged for a thousand years, devastating Skaro. The two sides started out with technologically advanced weapons, but a millennium of conflict all but exhausted the planet's resources and severely weakened both races. As the war drew to its conclusion, it descended into trench warfare, fought with ancient projectile weapons, mortar bombs, land mines and gas shells. Ammunition was scarce; so was manpower, and teenage soldiers were conscripted by generals who were not much older. The two civilisations were on the point of collapse.

Each side had by now retreated into their cities, shielded by massive protective domes, and were pouring their limited resources into research to produce weapons that would end the war. The Thals concentrated their efforts on the construction of a rocket, loaded with distronic explosives; the rocket would be fired at the enemy dome, destroying it and afflicting any Kaled survivors with distronic toxaemia. They were unaware that the Kaled Scientific Elite, working from a protected Bunker, had already developed a substance to reinforce their city's dome, giving it the strength of nine metres of concrete.

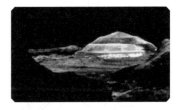

The Kaleds' chief scientist, Davros, had concluded that weapons research was by now futile. It was clear that Skaro's radiation-soaked air and environmentally devastated terrain were provoking irreversible genetic changes in his race, and Davros changed the direction of his research – instead of looking to win the war, he was seeking ways for the Kaleds to

survive it. He first experimented to discover his people's final mutated form, then devised a protective travel machine to house it.

Davros's ambition was for this new race – as he began to think of it – not merely to survive the carnage but to achieve supremacy by wiping out all other life on Skaro. Equipping the travel machines with weaponry for aggressive self-defence, he conducted further genetic experiments to isolate and remove those facets he believed to be fundamental weaknesses – compassion, any real sense of morality. To outlive all other races, Davros's new creatures would need to dominate – ruthlessly.

A few in the Scientific Elite were uneasy but powerless, unable to leave their Bunker or communicate with the Kaled government in the city. Those with qualms about Davros's aims were easily sidelined or removed by his security team. The genetic manipulation of the mutant embryos continued, and they were installed in the Mark III version of the new travel machines. Davros called his creation 'Dalek'. The name was an anagram of 'Kaled', reflecting the Dalek's mutation from its Kaled heritage.

When Davros gave them self-control, however, the Daleks quickly followed the logic of their programming. Reasoning that theirs was the only form of life that could be permitted to live, they turned on their creator and the Kaleds, killing them all. The Daleks now began the construction of Kalaann – a mighty new city of their own amidst the ruins of the destroyed Kaled city and the underground Bunker, with corridors, doors, elevators and walkways designed specifically for Dalek use.

There were, however, still significant numbers of Thal forces. They regrouped and, possibly recruiting Mutos, resumed hostilities against the Daleks. From secure levels beneath their city, the Daleks exploded a neutron bomb, finally ending the war.

# THE DEAD PLANET

The neutron explosion left Skaro utterly devastated, on a scale surpassing even that of the ruinous conditions at the end of the war. The buildings of the new city remained intact, but the soil was rendered barren, plant life was petrified, and vast swathes of the planet were turned to arid plains. Animal life either perished in the carnage or its mutation was horrifically accelerated. The air was infused with deadly levels of radiation, making it all but impossible for anyone to survive. The Daleks, secure in their underground base, now ruled Skaro, yet they were unable to venture onto the planet's surface and enjoy their conquest.

**THE DALEKS**
**by Terry Nation**
Starring William
Hartnell as the Doctor
**First broadcast:**
21/12/1963–01/02/1964

Davros had identified just seven galaxies and concluded that Skaro was the only planet capable of supporting intelligent life. The Daleks were, therefore, to take their place as the supreme beings – of the planet Skaro. This limitation in Davros's thinking had unintended side effects: dependent for their motive power on static electricity drawn up into their casings from the metal floors of their city, they were unable to move beyond its walls. Over the next five hundred years, still uncertain whether any Thals had survived the neutron bomb, the Daleks focused on the security of their city and monitoring the slowly dropping radiation levels outside, while finding a way to liberate themselves from their protective casings. The unwitting intervention of the Doctor would change all that...

The Doctor's arrival on Skaro with his granddaughter Susan and her teachers, Ian Chesterton and Barbara Wright, gave the Daleks a glimpse of alien life beyond their home world. At first, the Daleks naturally assumed the four travellers were Thals who had survived the effects of radiation poisoning by developing an anti-radiation drug. Though they were wrong about the time travellers, the Daleks were correct in assuming that there were Thals still alive on Skaro. Over the centuries, the Thals' mutation had come full circle, and they had out-evolved the physical imperfections caused by the war. They

were also farmers and pacifists, the only indication of their earlier technical abilities being their development of anti-radiation drugs.

The Daleks secured a supply of these drugs but soon found that the chemicals were lethal to them. They concluded that radiation was now a necessity for their existence and planned to explode a second neutron bomb – rather than adapt to their environment, they would change their environment to suit themselves. The Doctor and Ian led a group of Thals in a two-pronged assault on the Dalek city. In what Thal legends later called 'the Dalek War', they managed both to avert the detonation of the bomb and to knock out the Daleks' power source. Deprived of static electricity, the Daleks powered down and were left inert and lifeless. It was, in the words of one Dalek, the end of its race.

It wasn't the end, of course. All that was needed to restore the Daleks was power. Perhaps they were inadvertently reawakened by the technologically inexpert Thals, or perhaps some expedition from another world revived them, by accident or design – spacecraft from the Morok Empire and from Earth are thought to have stumbled upon Skaro, and there are bound to have been others. Whoever was responsible, the Daleks were restored to life, and they awoke with a new purpose. Aware now that there were not just surviving Thals on Skaro but also life on other worlds, their aim became the conquest of all other beings in the universe.

### TRACKING DALEK TIMELINES

c.450 ▶▶ The thousand-year war ▶▶ c.1450
c.1450 ▶▶ The creation of the Daleks ▶▶ c.1450
c.1963 ▶▶ **The Dalek War** ▶▶ c.1963

These Daleks were more primitive and technologically limited than any others the Doctor has since encountered. They had an extensive monitoring system, but were only just finding ways to make it reach beyond the city. They were ignorant of other worlds, had no concept of space travel, and had no knowledge of the Doctor or his TARDIS. They were still hoping to find a way to dispense with their protective casings and reclaim Skaro's soil, and were growing vegetables in artificial sunlight.

The Doctor later guessed that these events took place 'millions of years in the future'; in fact, his attempt to return to 1960s London seems to have ended up in roughly the right time but the wrong location.

# DESIGNING AN ICON

When *The Daleks* went into pre-production in the autumn of 1963, BBC staff designer Raymond Cusick was assigned to the serial. As well as designing the sets for the petrified jungle and the Dalek city, Ray's brief included realising the new alien creatures described in Terry Nation's script:

> Standing in a half circle in front of them are four hideous machine-like creatures. They are legless, moving on a round base. They have no human features. A lens on a flexible shaft acts as an eye. Arms with mechanical grips for hands ... The creatures hold strange weapons in their hands.
>
> **THE DALEKS**
> by Terry Nation

Ray Cusick recalls being 'puzzled' by this description, and phoning Terry Nation for clarification. Nation mentioned a show he'd seen in London by the Georgia State Dancers: 'I'd seen it too,' says Ray. 'Terry said: "Do you remember the peasant dance when the girls come on in long dresses and they seem to glide around like they're on roller skates? That's how I think the Daleks should move."' Ray was relieved; *Doctor Who*'s Associate Producer Mervyn Pinfield 'had already suggested I got cardboard tubes – a large cardboard tube for the body and other cardboard tubes for the arms and legs and paint them all silver.'

Audiences at the time were very familiar with onscreen aliens being portrayed by men in rubber suits, a cliché that Ray Cusick and Terry Nation were both determined to avoid. From there, Ray followed 'a system of logic. I had a weekend to work something out. I realised these things were going to be in the studios all day, and it was going to be hot under the lights, and they weren't going to be mechanically operated as that would pack up just before recording. So, I thought, if it's a human being inside and they'll be in it all day, they may as well be sitting down. So I drew a chair, sketched a person on it and then drew the shape round that. That was how it began. They had to be able to see, so there was a mesh that they could see out of but you couldn't see into, which gave it the neck, and the ray gun and the arm fitted into place beneath that.' Ray also toyed briefly with the idea

of moving the Dalek by means of a tricycle inside the casing, although this proved too expensive; instead the operators propelled the casings on three castors.

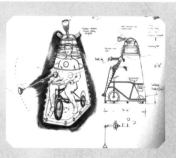

In October 1963, detailed plans were drawn up from these sketches by draughtsman A. Webb, from which Ray built a prototype Dalek with Jack Kine and Bernard Wilkie of the BBC Visual Effects department. This full-sized model was largely constructed out of wood and used an electric fan heater for the head. Outside contractors Shawcraft Models – who had only recently finished building the equally iconic TARDIS console – were given the task of building four working Dalek props following the Cusick-Kine-Wilkie example. Fibreglass replaced the timber of the prototype, and the whole casing was painted silver, with the exception of the hemispherical 'bumps' attached around the Daleks' lower sections. These were painted blue, after a plan to give them internal illumination was dropped: 'The blisters round the base of the Dalek were originally going to have lights connected to a car battery that would flash when they were agitated,' notes Ray, 'but we had to cut that as there were four Daleks and we couldn't afford four car batteries.'

A longstanding media legend states that the Daleks were inspired by pepper pots... 'Well if that's all it takes then anyone can be a designer! In reality, I took Bill Roberts at Shawcraft out to lunch and was telling him how I wanted them to move and I reached for the pepper pot and pushed it around to show him how I wanted it to move without any visible wheels or legs. Ever since, people have been saying I was inspired by the pepper pot, but I could just as easily reached for the salt cellar!'

Richard Martin, one of two directors working on *The Daleks*, was among the first people to see a working Dalek. 'I remember my first sight of them – we all went down to Shawcraft and went, "Yes!" They had that mechanised what's-out-there feel. The whole look was very successful.' Richard's one reservation concerned the sucker attachment: 'It was supposed to be able to suck anything – cloth, metal, people – but we ended up with an old sink plunger! It needed more money, but I was pleased with everything else.' The 'sink plunger' that had replaced Ray Cusick's original idea of mechanised claws was actually part of an arrangement of telescopic rods that could be manipulated by the operator to extend and retract on cue. A magnet was placed inside one of the suckers, which allowed the Dalek to hold a limited range of objects. They were equally inventive when it came to the eyestalk: 'Bill Roberts at Shawcraft said, "I've got an old iris from a camera that we can use in the eye, but I've got only one." So we used that for the close-ups.'

'Ray Cusick came up with these wonderful designs,' remembered *Doctor Who*'s first producer, Verity Lambert. 'I went down to rehearsal and we had the Dalek cases there – and everyone wanted to get in them and have a go, including me. I had no idea it was going to be that good, but there was just something about them.'

In rehearsal and in studio, the cast were initially sceptical: 'When we first saw the Daleks, we only saw half of them,' recalls Carole Ann Ford, who played the Doctor's granddaughter, Susan. 'We saw them in rehearsals with small men inside. How anyone could imagine they were ever going to be terrifying, I didn't know! But once they were in the studio and once that voice was attached to them, they were quite menacing. Whether it was the fact that they were this metallic box with who knows what inside, or whether it was that they were totally inhuman and therefore there was no reasoning with them, no point of contact… You just couldn't imagine what they were thinking.'

On their subsequent returns, Dalek design evolved with, for example, the addition of 'slats' above the midsections of their casings – intended by Ray Cusick as a new means for the Daleks to draw in power without the need for metal floors. But the changes were cosmetic: the essential look of the Daleks was immediately established, and has lasted almost five decades since.

Everyone involved at the time agrees that the original script laid only the groundwork for the classic design that followed. 'The rest Ray invented,' says Richard Martin, 'and he did it brilliantly.' As a BBC employee, however, Ray Cusick received only the standard BBC rate for his design work, although – some years later, when the iconic Dalek image had graced Technicolor movies, books, comic strips, slippers and tea towels – he was awarded an additional prize: a gold *Blue Peter* badge.

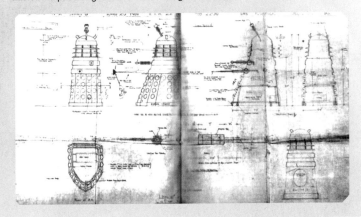

## First Encounters

Barbara hears the sound behind her and turns in time to see the thing advancing on her. Only its arms are seen by the audience as they pin Barbara's arm to her side and she starts to scream.

'You will move ahead of us and follow my directions.'

'So that's what a Dalek looks like.'

'Howdy, Mister! Say, you sure are an ugly-looking friend! ... My, my, boy, you've come all over in blue spots.'

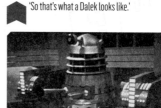

'Who are you? Who are you? Answer!'

# Do You Think There's Someone Inside Them?

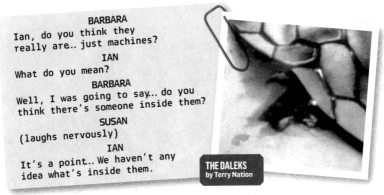

**BARBARA**
Ian, do you think they really are.. just machines?

**IAN**
What do you mean?

**BARBARA**
Well, I was going to say... do you think there's someone inside them?

**SUSAN**
(laughs nervously)

**IAN**
It's a point.. We haven't any idea what's inside them.

**THE DALEKS**
by Terry Nation

Each Dalek travel machine houses the artificially sustained remains of a Kaled in its ultimate mutated form. When the First Doctor and Ian opened the top of a captured Dalek, they discovered a grisly form that they quickly covered with a cloak. Deprived of life support and static power, the creature was dying, but it continued to strive to survive, a single webbed claw stretching out from beneath the cloak. Through the millennia that followed, even that 'final' mutated form was tampered with...

By the time the Seventh Doctor faced two Dalek factions in 1963 London, there were two distinct Dalek mutant forms:

The pure Kaled mutant was underdeveloped with vestigial limbs and almost amoeboid sensory organs.

Davros's new breed had functional appendages and some kind of mechanical prosthesis grafted into its body.

With the mutant creature removed, it is even possible for a humanoid to use the casing as a disguise.

## WELL, I WAS INSIDE THEM!

**DALEK OPERATORS** ▶▶ **Robert Jewell** (43 episodes, 1963–1969) ▶▶ **Kevin Manser** (31 episodes, 1963–1966) ▶▶ **Michael Summerton** (3 episodes, 1963–1964) ▶▶ **Gerald Taylor** (38 episodes, 1963–1967) ▶▶ **Nick Evans** (4 episodes, 1964) ▶▶ **Peter Murphy Grumbar** (25 episodes, 1964–1974) ▶▶ **John Scott Martin** (48 episodes, 1965–1988) ▶▶ **Ken Tyllsen** (1 episode, 1967) ▶▶ **Rick Newby** (4 episodes, 1972) ▶▶ **Cy Town** (25 episodes, 1973–1988) ▶▶ **Keith Ashley** (4 episodes, 1975) ▶▶ **Mike Mungarvan** (4 episodes, 1979) ▶▶ **Tony Starr** (7 episodes, 1984–1988) ▶▶ **Toby Byrne** (4 episodes, 1984–1985) ▶▶ **Hugh Spight** (4 episodes, 1988) ▶▶ **Barnaby Edwards** (12 episodes, 2005–2010) ▶▶ **Nicholas Pegg** (9 episodes, 2005–2010) ▶▶ **David Hankinson** (8 episodes, 2005–2008) ▶▶ **Anthony Spargo** (6 episodes, 2006–2008) ▶▶ **Dan Barratt** (2 episodes, 2006) ▶▶ **Stuart Crossman** (2 episodes, 2006) ▶▶ **Ben Ashley** (2 episodes, 2010) ▶▶ **Jon Davey** (1 episode, 2010) ▶▶ **Mathew Doman** (1 episode, 2010) ▶▶ **Joe White** (1 episode, 2010) ▶▶ **Jeremy Harvey** (1 episode, 2010) ▶▶ **Sean Saye** (1 episode, 2010)

John Scott Martin

Barnaby Edwards

# VOICING AN ICON

The Daleks' otherworldly electronic speech was created by actors Peter Hawkins and David Graham, who devised the harsh monotone of their staccato delivery which they then enhanced using a ring modulator, in collaboration with members of the BBC Radiophonic Workshop, including Dick Mills.

Except that there wasn't really one distinctive Dalek voice, as the current Voice of the Daleks, Nicholas Briggs, explains: 'We didn't really get to what we now recognise as the Dalek Voice until about *The Daleks' Master Plan*. Until then, Hawkins was just experimenting and finding out what worked. I once asked Dick Mills why the early Dalek voices varied so much, and he said, "We never wrote the settings down." So almost every Dalek story right until 2005 has a different voice. It's amazing the effect a slightly different setting on the ring modulator has.'

Hawkins and Graham established a working method where one would speak in a lower, gruff pitch, and the other would be pitched higher. 'Peter Hawkins gave the Black Daleks this maniacal really high voice,' notes Nicholas. 'And David Graham did a fantastic job adding a sort of creepiness and weirdness to the Dalek voice. In *The Chase* you get comedy Daleks – you even get the Dalek who can't count. You can look back on it now and think, "That's ridiculous, Daleks don't behave like that," but at the time they were trying new ideas... although they didn't do it again!'

## What Is a Ring Modulator?

A ring modulator is an engineering component that was first used in the early days of radio and telephony. It combines two signals into one, and can also be used to decode those two signals again. Imagine a transmitter adding two radio stations together into a single signal that is then decoded again by the receiving radio set. Combining the actor saying 'Exterminate' with an electrical tone generated at a certain frequency produces the Dalek sound, which can in theory be separated again.

**DALEK VOICES** ▶▶ Peter Hawkins (41 episodes, 1963–1967) ▶▶ David Graham (29 episodes, 1963–1966) ▶▶ Roy Skelton (24 episodes, 1967–1988) ▶▶ Oliver Gilbert (4 episodes, 1972) ▶▶ Peter Messaline (4 episodes, 1972) ▶▶ Michael Wisher (10 episodes, 1973–1974) ▶▶ David Gooderson (4 episodes, 1979) ▶▶ Brian Miller (5 episodes, 1984–1988) ▶▶ Royce Mills (7 episodes, 1984–1988) ▶▶ Geoffrey Sax (1 episode, 1996) ▶▶ Nicholas Briggs (12 episodes, 2005–2010)

## DIRECTING AN ICON

'Christopher Barry did the first few episodes of *The Daleks*, and then I became the Dalek Director for well over a year,' recalls Richard Martin.

'The hardest thing about directing Daleks was making them mobile, which we never quite did! They were very leaden pieces of equipment. Those poor, poor people inside – they were very cramped and they had to pedal like crazy and they were only on castors. I was never happy with the way they moved. It would have been nice to have had them electronically operated by remote control, but the technology wasn't good enough at the time: if we had used it in the studio it wouldn't have been reliable. It was more reliable to have little men inside them, hoping that they would go in the right direction.

'When you were shooting Daleks, you had to go in low or shoot up high, or swing round them to give them a dynamic they themselves did not possess. The Daleks sometimes had to find their marks on the floor which was very difficult to see through the gauze. To help them, we numbered them.

'In *The Chase*, we had a stupid Dalek, a fearful Dalek – they all had to obey, but maybe some didn't want to obey because they were fearful. I felt that there was a moment when you could almost have felt sorry for a Dalek – that this thing, once humanoid, had reduced itself to a blob of jelly in a bit of tin, but it still thought of itself as human, with a soul and an intelligence, while that intelligence had become warped by the very nature of their confinement.'

## DALEKMANIA

### The Dalek Book

On 30 June 1964, five months before the Daleks' second television appearance, Dalek fans were treated to the lavishly illustrated publication *The Dalek Book* – one of the earliest items of *Doctor Who* merchandise to be produced. *The Dalek Book* was the first of three annual-style books and was followed by *The Dalek World* (1965) and *The Dalek Outer Space Book* (1966). All three contained a series of full-colour comic strips and text stories, telling the linked story of the Dalek Emperor's attempts to invade the Earth, the surrender of the Daleks, and their various plans to escape.

Readers thrilled to stories of flying Daleks, Marsh Daleks and battles with Mechonoids. In one remarkable story, an Earth pilot manages to make his way inside the beautifully drawn city of Skaro, where he discovers that Daleks burp and claim to have invented Shakespeare. He also sneaks away with a drawing of the insides of a Dalek – a coup for 1964. Later stories also made use of the Space Security Service and its agent Sara Kingdom, tying in with the 1965 TV stories *Mission to the Unknown* and *The Daleks' Master Plan*. But the real star of these books was the gold Dalek Emperor – a figure who soon rose to great prominence in *The Dalek Chronicles* (see p.31).

In amongst this Dalek gold were several slightly more bizarre features – such as the story where a Dalek invasion was defeated by a garden mole, and a photo story where Susan returned to Skaro and terrified the Daleks with her laughter. The books contained a wealth of fascinating Dalek information: Daleks could not see the colour red; there was a continent on Skaro called Darren; Daleks communicated using the Dalekode...

The books were predominantly the work of Terry Nation and script editor David Whitaker, and both also worked on *The Dalek Pocketbook and Space Traveller's Guide* (1965), much of which is a retelling of 'The Dalek Cubes', a series of history files about the Daleks which Nation claimed to have found in his garden. The retelling is in the form of a Q and A, a sample of which goes:

*Q: Dare they tamper with the forces of creation?*
*TERRY: Yes they dare.*

## Doctor Who in an Exciting Adventure with the Daleks

In 1964, David Whitaker wrote what turned out to be the first novel in a record-breaking range of books that has continued for almost half a century. Naturally, the series began with the Daleks: *Doctor Who in an Exciting Adventure with the Daleks* was published on 12 November 1964 and retold the Doctor's first encounter with his deadliest enemies, but from Ian Chesterton's point of view. The first edition (and later reprints) featured illustrations by Arnold Schwartzman, while a 1965 paperback version was illustrated by Peter Archer. Capitalising on the chance to start again, Whitaker includes a broad reimagining of *Doctor Who*'s first ever episode, then skips over the three episodes set in Earth's prehistory to launch straight into his adaptation of the first Dalek serial. It is

a gripping adventure story taking the reader from Skaro's petrified jungle to the Dalek City and the Lake of Mutations.

Along the way, Whitaker indulges his love of embellishing Dalek culture. The creatures are depicted with a variety of attachments, there is a hydro-electric plant and, most significant of all, the Daleks are ruled by a Glass Dalek. Peter Archer's accompanying illustration shows this Glass Dalek containing a much less mutated creature, wearing a stolen TARDIS fluid link around his neck. Whitaker had now introduced the idea of the Daleks having a hierarchy – but he had an even better notion around the corner...

*I jumped to one side as it fired at me*

# WORLD'S END

Once they realised there was life on other planets, the Daleks developed spaceships in order to invade them. They became capable of interstellar travel with terrifying speed: a couple of centuries after their defeat by the Thals and the Doctor, the Daleks were swarming through their galaxy and beyond.

**THE DALEK INVASION OF EARTH**
by Terry Nation
Starring William Hartnell as the Doctor
**First broadcast:**
21/11/1964–26/12/1964

Their tactics followed a consistent pattern: in a chilling echo of the thousand-year war, each planet would be bombarded with bacteria-carrying meteorite showers, unleashing a plague that killed millions and weakened the remaining inhabitants, splitting them into small, isolated communities. A few months after the bacteria barrage, the Dalek saucers would arrive. The debilitated population would be unable to offer serious resistance and there would be mass exterminations followed by ruthless suppression of the survivors, who

would become a slave workforce, often in the Daleks' extensive mining operations. Supervised by Robomen, the subjugated people were set to work in the Dalek mine-works that plundered each planet's resources.

The Daleks selected Earth for an audacious new plan to tamper with the very forces of creation. The operation was designated 'Project De-Gravitate': Earth's core would be replaced with a power system, allowing the Daleks to pilot the planet anywhere in the universe. The Doctor, Ian, Barbara and Susan joined forces with London's resistance fighters and managed to prevent the Daleks' fission capsule from reaching the Earth's core. The Dalek command saucer was caught up in the ensuing explosion, signalling the end of the Dalek invasion of Earth.

## Robomen

The Robomen were human slaves of the Daleks who had been altered and turned into crude cyborgs. The Dalek selection process for robotisation required a high level of intelligence determined by one of a series of intelligence tests, but once humans were converted, little trace remained of their original personalities. Selected subjects were anaesthetised, then robotised on an operating table fitted inside each Dalek saucer.

The process had a relatively high failure rate, probably because the necessary brain surgery was very invasive and the Daleks had little interest in their subjects'

### TRACKING DALEK TIMELINES

c.1450 ❱❱ The creation of the Daleks ❱❱ c.1450
c.1963 ❱❱ The Dalek War ❱❱ c.1963
2157 ❱❱ The Dalek invasion of Earth ❱❱ 2167

The Daleks' earliest known means of escaping their city's confines was the power receiver attached to the rear of the casing. This new-found mobility paved the way for interplanetary conquest.

The Doctor and Ian discovered a makeshift calendar dated '2164' in an abandoned warehouse near Battersea. While aboard the Dalek saucer at Chelsea, they learned from a fellow prisoner that the meteorite bombardment had occurred ten years earlier. Much later, the Doctor confirmed that the Daleks had invaded Earth in 2157.

survival. Following successful conversion, the remaining lifespan of a Roboman was in any case quite short. Converted Robomen wore a cumbersome helmet through which Dalek orders were conveyed directly into their brains. Removal of the helmets resulted in death, and some Robomen experienced a brief return to human consciousness before dying. The Dalek conditioning was also unreliable, and some Robomen regained a semblance of original thought. They were driven insane by the knowledge of what had been done to them: some smashed their heads against walls; some threw themselves off buildings, and their drowned bodies were sometimes found floating in local waterways.

# DALEK HIERARCHY

## Saucer Commander

During a planetary invasion, each Dalek saucer was under the command of a taskforce leader, distinguishable by its black dome and the alternating dark and light vertical panels of its lower section. The taskforce leader took its instructions from Dalek Supreme Command on the occupied planet.

## Black Dalek

A Black Dalek was the Supreme Controller of each planetary invasion force, and was part of a whole tier of Dalek commanders. The leader of the Earth invasion was based at the mining operation in Bedfordshire, where it was regarded by its human slaves as a concentration camp commandant; this was actually Dalek Supreme Command and directed all Dalek activity on the planet. This Black Dalek was destroyed in the volcanic eruption that ended the invasion. A Black Dalek commanded the time-travel operation to pursue and exterminate the Doctor in the wake of Project De-Gravitate. On the Dalek home world, the Black Daleks reported to the Emperor and relayed orders to the drones in the rest

of the city. One of their rank was designated the Dalek Supreme and led Dalek Supreme Command. The Dalek Supreme directed operations on the planet Kembel and headed the Galactic Council the Dalek had established. If the Dalek Supreme was destroyed, its place was taken by another Black Dalek.

## The Dalek Chronicles

In the 1960s, *TV Century 21* was a popular weekly children's magazine featuring the comic strip adventures of popular characters from science fiction TV series made by Gerry Anderson, such as *Stingray*, *Fireball XL5* and *Thunderbirds*. Its first issue was published on 23 January 1965 and included the first of 104 instalments of *The Daleks by Terry Nation*. These strips were chiefly written by David Whitaker (and approved by Nation), and were illustrated by Richard Jennings, Ron Turner or Eric Eden. Jennings had already been responsible for the comic strips in *The Dalek Book*, and the *TVC21* strips followed a similar format and continuity. The stories were bold and imaginative, featuring exploding planets, whole Dalek fleets in battle, and gloriously ambitious ideas.

*The Daleks* didn't feature the Doctor – the strip was purely about the adventures of the Daleks, from their creation by the dying blue-skinned Skaroene scientist Yarvelling through to their emergence as a conquering space fleet led by the magnificent Gold Dalek Emperor. It told the story of the Daleks' triumph over many setbacks – from the near-total destruction of their city on Skaro and several battles with the Mechonoids to the beginnings of their earliest attack on planet Earth. The Daleks meet (and exterminate) creatures worse than themselves, but they are not depicted as heroes – they are shown to enslave and destroy magnificent civilisations, while the Gold Emperor hatches various cruel plans. There is also a whole new side to Dalek culture – it is not uncommon for the Daleks to have names and freedom of thought – a notion that would not really find its place on television until the arrival of the Cult of Skaro in 2006 (see p.117). Dalek Sec is foreshadowed in the comic strips by a Dalek called Zeg, who becomes the first Dalek to be 'infected' with an independent spirit, and challenges the Emperor for supremacy, an idea David Whitaker would return to in 1967...

# FLIGHT THROUGH ETERNITY

**THE CHASE**
by Terry Nation
Starring William
Hartnell as the Doctor
**First broadcast:**
22/05/1965–22/06/1965

Back on Skaro, the Daleks made immediate plans to eliminate the Doctor, whom they now identified as their greatest enemy, having matched reports from Earth with the data they held on his earlier visit to Skaro. The Daleks now had a prototype, dimensionally transcendental time-travel craft. Its first mission: to hunt down the TARDIS.

The Daleks pursued the Doctor from the desert world of Aridius, taking in various points in Earth's history, before cornering him on the planet Mechanus. A robot duplicate of the Doctor was used to infiltrate the TARDIS crew, but its programming was out of date – the Daleks were unaware that the Doctor's granddaughter had stayed on Earth after the invasion, and the duplicate revealed itself by wrongly identifying the Doctor's new companion Vicki as Susan.

The Daleks had no further opportunity to capture or kill their enemy, because Mechanus was the adopted home of a robot race, the Mechonoids. The Mechonoid city was destroyed in the ensuing battle, and the Doctor and his friends escaped.

## TRACKING DALEK TIMELINES

c.1963 ▶▶ The Dalek War ▶▶ c.1963
2157 ▶▶ The Dalek invasion of Earth ▶▶ 2167
c.2167 ▶▶ The pursuit of the Doctor ▶▶ c.2265

The Daleks had now devised a new means of travelling without dependency on metal floors – an internal power supply generated from energy drawn via sensor plates positioned above the midsections of their casings, the last significant alteration to their external appearance for a couple of thousand years.

The chase began very shortly after Skaro received reports of the failure of the Earth conquest, and the Daleks followed the Doctor to Ancient New York (1966), the Mary Celeste (1872) and the Festival of Ghana (1996). The Mechonoids' captive, Steven Taylor, was a pilot in Earth's earliest space exploration programmes in the 23rd to 25th centuries.

## Mechonoids

The Mechonoids were seemingly widely used at an early stage of Earth's colonisation programme, and the Daleks had encountered them before arriving on Mechanus. Designed by Earth scientists to help colonise other worlds, they were a robot race – geometric spheres, equipped with flame throwers and manipulation appendages. They spoke in a series of simple commands. A force of Mechonoids would be dispatched to a planet, where they would construct vast cities, which they were programmed to defend ruthlessly while they awaited the arrival of Earth colonists.

The first such world was named Mechanus. Its expected colonists never arrived and so, in the absence of any other orders, the Mechonoids formed their own society. When they finally encountered an Earthman, the astronaut Steven Taylor, they would not accept his orders. Instead, they they kept him as a specimen or pet.

## DALEKMANIA

### The Big Screen

In 1965 and 1966, two Dalek movies were made by film-maker Milton Subotsky, liberally adapting the first two Dalek stories for cinema screens. These were remarkably lavish productions in comparison with the budgetary restrictions of their television parent, featuring up to eighteen brightly coloured Dalek props in sumptuous Technicolor settings.

Legendary movie star Peter Cushing played the *Tardis*-inventor Dr Who, accompanied by various members of his family – his granddaughters Susan Who (Roberta Tovey) and Barbara Who (Jennie Linden) and his niece Louise (Jill Curzon). Roy Castle played Ian in the first film; Bernard Cribbins was his successor, · Tom, in the second.

The films were well received. *Dr Who and the Daleks* was a fairly faithful 80-minute version of the first television Dalek story, dominated by a very impressive version of the

Dalek city. Where the original had reflected the claustrophobic nature of its inhabitants, these Daleks were enormous and lived in grand halls linked by imposingly sweeping corridors.

A larger budget for the second film

# SPACE WARS

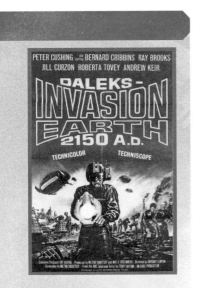

PETER CUSHING starring BERNARD CRIBBINS · RAY BROOKS
JILL CURZON · ROBERTA TOVEY · ANDREW KEIR

**DALEKS-
INVASION
EARTH
2150 A.D.**

TECHNICOLOR          TECHNISCOPE

allowed the producers to make the most of the story of *The Dalek Invasion of Earth*. Renamed *Daleks – Invasion Earth 2150 AD*, the film featured a stunning alien spaceship, extensive location filming around London, striking Dalek voices and impressive costumes for the Robomen. The film features a notably more dramatic denouement than its TV source – the Daleks are sucked into the Earth's core.

One of the few things not reproduced on screen was the famous Dalek negative gun effect from the television. Instead, the Daleks were equipped with guns that fired white clouds of carbon dioxide gas. Although these were fired copiously in the first film, audiences complained that the Daleks only killed one person – something enthusiastically corrected in the second film.

Fondly remembered, TV screenings of these films were for years the only way of seeing a version of the first two Dalek adventures. Subotsky never exercised his option to make a third Dalek film.

Throughout the third millennium, the Dalek conquest of the universe continued, though it would be some centuries before they would make another attempt on Earth itself. By the 26th century, Earth's own empire had expanded, bringing humans into contact with a reptilian race from the planet Draconia. The Draconian empire was as extensive as Earth's, and the two powers clashed briefly before establishing an uneasy peace. When the Daleks attacked, Earth and Draconia fought back – a period that became known as the Dalek Wars (see p.55). The outermost planets of Earth's empire were subjected to chemical bombardment, the resultant plague curable only with a rare mineral known as parrinium. The Daleks despatched taskforces to any world with parrinium deposits to prevent Earth getting hold of the cure. One such world was Exxilon, where a living city drained the Daleks' power supplies and an Earth mission to mine parrinium ended in catastrophe (see pp.60).

The Dalek Wars eventually ended with another short-lived invasion of Earth followed by a tactical retreat from the Milky Way around the year 3000. For the next 500 years or so, humanity saw little or no Dalek activity but, from 3500 to 4000, Earth's Space Security Service observed closely as the Daleks gained control of over 70 planets in the Ninth Galactic System and 40 more in the Constellation of Miros, among them the planet Kembel...

# THE DESTRUCTION OF TIME

📺 **MISSION TO THE UNKNOWN**
by Terry Nation
Starring William
Hartnell as the Doctor
**First broadcast:**
09/10/1965

**THE DALEKS' MASTER PLAN**
by Terry Nation and
Dennis Spooner
Starring William
Hartnell as the Doctor
**First broadcast:**
13/11/1965–29/01/1966

In the year 4000, the Daleks formed an unlikely pact with several major galactic forces, all hostile to the Earth empire. The Daleks organised a series of intergalactic conferences, often coinciding with similar summit meetings attended by Earth's rulers. The sixth and seventh conferences were held on the planet Kembel, where the delegates were joined by the final member of their council – Mavic Chen, the Guardian of Earth's solar system. The ambitious Chen supplied an emm of the rare mineral taranium, essential to the construction of the Daleks' latest weapon. The Time Destructor was the first Dalek weapon intended to annihilate non-Dalek life across the cosmos on an inconceivable scale.

The Dalek plan was disrupted by the arrival of the Doctor, who fled with the taranium core. Once again, the Daleks pursued the Doctor through space and time, eventually cornering him in Ancient Egypt and forcing him to surrender the taranium core. Back on Kembel, however, the Doctor turned the Time Destructor on the Dalek forces, which were completely destroyed.

**TRACKING DALEK TIMELINES**
2540 ➤➤ The Dalek Wars ➤➤ c.3000
3000 ➤➤ The Daleks regroup and prepare ➤➤ 4000
4000 ➤➤ The Galactic Alliance ➤➤ 4000

The non-aggression pact of 3975 brought a quarter-century of peace to the Milky Way, a fact celebrated by Mavic Chen, the Guardian of the Solar System, in an interview on Earth's Channel 403 news. Shortly after giving this interview, Chen arrived on Kembel to take his place in the Dalek alliance against Earth.

## Mavic Chen

Mavic Chen was the Guardian of the
Solar System in the late 40th century.
A popular ruler with a strong grasp
on the media, none of his subjects
suspected that for 50 years he had
been working as part of the Dalek
alliance, secretly harvesting a full
emm of taranium on the outer planets

in order to power the Daleks' Time Destructor. Despite signing up to the
non-aggression pact of 3975, in the year 4000 Chen announced he was
taking a holiday and flew to the planet Kembel in his Spar 740 spaceship,
taking the taranium to the Dalek alliance.

Chen was hoping to use the Daleks to become the supreme ruler of the
universe, but to the Daleks he was simply a tool – when the Doctor stole
the taranium core, Chen was dispatched to recover it. Chen rapidly became
insane, finally challenging the Dalek Supreme for control of the Daleks, at
which point he was exterminated.

## The Galactic Council

The Daleks gathered together an alliance of powerful empires and races, yet most of them seem to have contributed little to the Daleks' plan. It's possible that the Daleks had calculated that their own attack on Earth's solar system would be more

likely to succeed if they had already neutralised any rival powers. Rather than commit resources and fleets to overcoming the dominant powers of a number of other systems and galaxies, the Daleks lured their rulers into an illusory alliance. Then, when the delegates gathered for their final meeting before the invasion, they were to be disposed of. When this failed, the surviving delegates united against the Daleks.

**ALIEN DELEGATES** ▶▶ Mavic Chen, Guardian of the Solar System ▶▶ Gearon ▶▶ Trantis ▶▶ Malpha ▶▶ Beaus ▶▶ Sentreal ▶▶ Warrien ▶▶ Celation ▶▶ Zephon, Master of the Fifth Galaxy

# DALEKMANIA

## The Curse of the Daleks

In December 1965, avid *Doctor Who* fans faced a tough choice: stay at home and watch the latest thrilling episode of *The Daleks' Master Plan*, or go to Wyndham's Theatre to see the Daleks live on the London stage.

*The Curse of the Daleks* was credited to David Whitaker and Terry Nation and worked as a sort of sequel to the first Dalek story, explaining how a visiting group of Earthmen re-awoke the original Daleks, while a mysterious figure supplied them with a new power source. Set in broadly the same world as *The Dalek Book*, the play featured courageous rocket captains, coolly independent female scientists, untrustworthy criminals and noble Thals. It offered a mixture of deep-space adventure, murder mystery and epic Dalek action, ending in an exciting battle, with the humans triumphing, but being warned: 'The Daleks are waiting...'

Plans for a possible tour were eventually dropped, and the production was never revived.

For many years it was almost entirely forgotten until, in 2008, Michael Praed starred in an audio adaptation by Big Finish Productions.

# WE HAVE CHANGED THE PATTERN OF HISTORY!

W hen a small taskforce left Skaro in one of the dimensionally transcendental time craft, it crash-landed on the planet Vulcan millennia earlier. The capsule sank into a mercury swamp, but was recovered after a couple of centuries by Lesterson, a scientist in a newly settled human colony. Displaying their usual cunning, the Daleks promptly

📺 **THE POWER OF THE DALEKS**
by David Whitaker
Starring Patrick
Troughton as the Doctor
**First broadcast:**
05/11/1966–10/12/1966

assumed the guise of willing servants, while secretly securing the power supply that would enable them to begin to build a new race of Daleks. The Doctor's arrival put an end to this scheme, though not before countless human colonists had died in a Dalek-manipulated uprising.

## THE END OF THE DALEKS

In the wake of the Time Destructor disaster, the Daleks began to experiment with time-corridor technology. The Dalek Emperor quickly saw an opportunity to combine revenge on his race's greatest enemy with the total subjugation of Earth in every era. Rather than conquer the planet, the

Daleks would instil the Dalek Factor in all of humanity throughout history, and the Doctor's ultimate humiliation would be to identify and distribute the Dalek Factor himself.

The Emperor devised a complex scheme to inveigle the Doctor into an investigation spanning a century that would entice him into synthesising the Dalek Factor. Tracking the TARDIS, the Daleks discovered that the Doctor had undergone his first regeneration. Establishing a stable link between 41st-century Skaro and Victorian England, they enlisted the help of two 19th-century Englishmen – playing on the avarice of one and the fear and compassion of the other – to lure the Doctor into conducting an experiment supposedly designed to reveal the qualities that made up the Human Factor, but with the Dalek Factor as its actual end goal.

**THE EVIL OF THE DALEKS**
by David Whitaker
Starring Patrick Troughton as the Doctor
**First broadcast:** 20/05/1967–01/07/1967

The Doctor introduced the Human Factor into three Daleks, which he named Alpha, Beta and Omega. These humanised Daleks were childlike and playful, and soon began questioning the orders of the Black Daleks. Grasping the implications of any dissent among his Daleks, the Emperor agreed to the Doctor's suggestion that all Daleks should pass through the conversion machinery so that the humanised Daleks would revert to their Dalek selves. But the Doctor had tampered with the conversion device and the Human Factor was soon spreading through the Dalek race. As increasing numbers of Dalek drones defied their orders and turned against the Black Daleks, civil war broke out in the city, and the last thing the Doctor saw before leaving Skaro was the Emperor himself under fire in his control room. This, the Doctor believed, would be the Daleks' final end.

### TRACKING DALEK TIMELINES

4000 ➤➤ The Galactic Alliance ➤➤ 4000
41st century ➤➤ Dalek Civil War ➤➤ 41st century
41st century ➤➤ Timeship flees Skaro and crashes on Vulcan ➤➤ 21st century

Vulcan's Earth base was one of humanity's first non-terrestrial colonies; the human settlers were unfamiliar with the machine creatures they'd discovered, so Earth had yet to be invaded. But the Daleks were from a later period – the Doctor had regenerated immediately before his arrival on Vulcan, yet the stranded Daleks recognised him, presumably from their monitoring of his travels prior to the Civil War on Skaro in the far future.

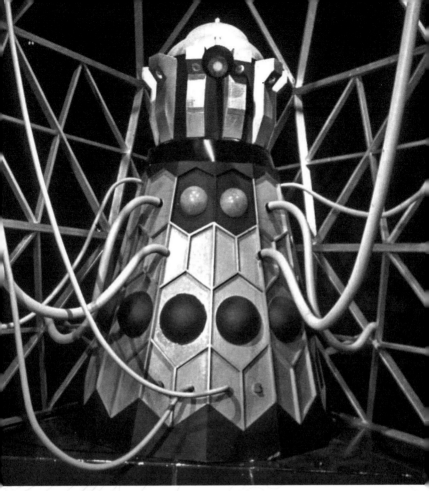

# DALEK HIERARCHY

## The Dalek Emperor

The ruler of the Daleks was housed in a giant immobile casing at the heart of Kalaann. Cables linked his casing to the city's power and data sources, through which he could monitor and control Dalek activity – the vast brain at the centre of the Dalek civilisation. He was protected and served by black-domed Dalek guards, which obeyed his orders and reported on the success of his plans.

The Doctor and the Emperor were aware of each other for many years, but they didn't meet until the Emperor ordered the theft of the TARDIS and set in train his Dalek Factor stratagem. They would meet again – millennia later and in another timeline…

## The Dalek Factor

The Dalek Factor is an instinctive, unthinking mixture of hatred and obedience. A true Dalek cannot hide its disgust for all other life forms, which stems from its own self-loathing.

Daleks are incapable of seeing the good in another species – only elements of themselves that they recognise. They are skilled manipulators, understanding the weaknesses of lesser species and how to play to them, which makes them excellent at forming temporary alliances.

Daleks obey without question. When Dalek Omega questioned an order, the sedition was so alarming it was immediately reported to the Emperor Dalek; like the Doctor, the Emperor quickly recognised the imminence of civil war on Skaro. Daleks understand that they must obey, frequently restating their agreement. Daleks do not engage in conversation, as such, merely the issuing of orders, the agreement to follow them and the repetition of these orders as a mantra. A Dalek without orders is without purpose.

When the Doctor first visited Skaro, he saw vestigial traces of their Kaled heritage – metal sculptures placed around the city – but this was the sole example of the Daleks having something that was not purely functional. Dalek spaceships have always been extremely utilitarian, both inside and out.

It is true that the Daleks learn from their mistakes, but it is more accurate to say that they learn from the mistakes of other Daleks. At the time of the Doctor's first visit to Skaro, the Daleks poisoned by the

Thals' anti-radiation drug were simply sealed up in Section 3 of the Dalek city without further thought. Failure is not an option.

Individually, Daleks have little sense of self. They perform acts of clinical self-sacrifice for the greater Dalek cause, which masks the real, emotional nature of the Dalek creature inside the casing. When under attack, Daleks will panic, scream and call for help. If the eyestalk on the casing is impaired, the lack of external vision immediately sends the occupant into a frenzy. Similarly, Daleks can feel pain and often cry out in agony when they are dying. On rare occasions they will beg for pity or mercy, despite claiming not to have the word in their vocabulary banks.

# 'NO MORE THAN THREE DALEKS TO BE SEEN TOGETHER AT ANY ONE TIME!'

*Doctor Who* has never had enough Daleks. These days, computer-generated imagery (CGI) can produce swarms of Daleks to supplement the working props whenever required. But in earlier times, budgets, schedules and technical limitations stimulated the production team to devise ingenious ways to portray armies of Daleks...

For the first serial, four fully operational Daleks were constructed by Shawcraft Models. Directors Christopher Barry and Richard Martin used careful camerawork to suggest that there were more Daleks in a scene simply by showing the same prop from different angles. Another trick was to start a scene with all four Daleks in it, then despatch a Dalek to the next set ready for the next scene. This story also saw the use of crowd Daleks – life-size photographs placed in the background of the set. *The Dalek Invasion of Earth* (1964) introduced a black Dalek, which was repainted slightly between episodes to represent the difference between a Saucer Commander and the Black Dalek who ran the mines.

For *The Chase* (1965), Richard Martin hit upon the idea of trying to swell Dalek forces further with a 'Dalek Merry-Go-Round' – having the Daleks leave through a door and then hurriedly wheel round the set to go through the same door again. The production team also secured some props from the Dalek films – these were hurriedly reconditioned and placed in the background, noticeably lacking their bases. As the 1960s wore on, bits of these Daleks were mixed and matched, repaired and repainted.

The merry-go-round technique was repeated in *The Power of the Daleks* (1966) to suggest a Dalek production line. Christopher Barry also reused the life-size photographic Daleks in the background – although a draught in the studio caused them to sway gently during their scenes. Christopher also capitalised on Dalekmania, cheaply populating his production-line footage with dozens of toy Daleks. A cunningly scripted line from the Dalek leader avoided having to show the new Dalek army swarming around the colony: 'No more than three Daleks to be seen together at any one time!'

In *The Evil of the Daleks* (1967), a clever mixture of live action, model filming and a toy massacre conveyed the final destruction of Skaro's Dalek city. By *Day of the Daleks* (1972), only three working props remained in BBC hands. Since one was now painted gold, Jon Pertwee pointed out, it was quite obvious when three of them were trying to look like an army. For *Planet of the Daleks* (1973), several 'Goon Daleks' were built – dummies that were occasionally rocked by stagehands to suggest movement. Toys were also used to create the frozen army of 10,000 Daleks. A 1960s movie Dalek, borrowed from Terry Nation, became the Dalek Supreme.

*Destiny of the Daleks* (1979) saw four working Daleks hurriedly assembled out of bits and pieces (including a prop from a travelling exhibition that looked very little like a Dalek). These four Daleks were accompanied on location filming by a horde of lightweight vacuum-formed dummy casings. Some were only single-sided half-Daleks, and were carried through the Skaro wastelands by extras; the end effect was less of a glide and more of a bounce. Most of these were blown up on location. By the time the four real Dalek props made it back into the studio, they had suffered considerable damage. There wasn't time to repair them properly, so Tom Baker's Doctor was menaced by Daleks with bits missing or, in one case, held together with tape.

Advances in manufacturing processes allowed the building of four new props for both *Revelation of the Daleks* (1985) and *Remembrance of the Daleks* (1988), which introduced the cream and gold Imperial Daleks. Clever direction allowed the series to present the spectacle of large numbers of opposing Dalek factions engaging in a full-scale war.

# THE RE-ANIMATION OF THE DALEKS

*The Power of the Daleks* is one of several 1960s *Doctor Who* serials no longer held in the BBC Archives. In 2005, BBC Online animated two missing episodes from another lost 1960s story, *The Invasion*. A follow-up project to animate *The Power of the Daleks* was considered, and a trailer was made for BBC Online by Firestep, the team behind *The Invasion*.

# DALEKMANIA

In 1963 and 1964, as The Beatles went from pop hit to cultural phenomenon, an inventive journalist coined the term 'Beatlemania'. Ever since, the press has been on the lookout for the latest craze and has frequently reached for that -*mania* suffix. 'Dalekmania' was one of the earliest examples of that. It was originally used in British newspapers in the mid 1960s. Since their first television appearance, the Daleks had been massively popular among the nation's schoolchildren, and playgrounds were reportedly full of kids impersonating Daleks. The non-commercial BBC was fairly slow to exploit this popularity, as producer Verity Lambert recalled:

'Dalekmania started with the first serial, and *The Dalek Invasion of Earth* consolidated it. The BBC then sold off the merchandising rights to a man called Walter Tuckwell. I and some girlfriends were in a restaurant one day, and there was only one other table in the restaurant, and we got chatting to them and introduced ourselves. When I said my name, this man said, "You have made me a millionaire!" It was Walter Tuckwell. I was earning £1,600 a year at this time, so I said to him, "Well, the least you can do is take me out to dinner." So he arrived in his Bentley one evening.'

Dalek merchandise began to appear in 1964 – *The Dalek Book*, the first novel, a couple of badges, a very scarce Dalek dressing-up kit – but it was in 1965 that the Daleks really exploded into high-street stores. Suddenly there were activity books and annuals, masks and slippers, novelty sweets, cakes and Easter eggs, fireworks and candles, jigsaws, sponges and soap, children's crockery and picnic sets, greetings cards and stationery, anti-Dalek water pistols, snow globes, wallpaper and

balloons... For *Doctor Who* fans, there'd be nothing like it again until 2005.

1965 also saw the release of more than forty different models, action figures and playsets. The most popular models were the Rolykin and Louis Marx Daleks – a Rolykin Dalek could be bought for the price of a packet of sweets. Other options included the Swap-It Daleks, which came in a range of coloured pieces, allowing owners of several to mix-and-match to create their very own multicoloured Daleks.

As director Richard Martin points out, the toys were not perfect: 'They were inaccurate.

**800 Battery-operated Dalek**
6" tall. Individually boxed. Packed one dozen. 123/6 per dozen.
Retail 17/11

**540 Friction Sparking Dalek**
6½" tall. Individually boxed. Packed one dozen per carton in assorted colours. 89/- per dozen.
Retail 12/11

**8350 Dalek Rolykin**
Only 1" tall. Individually boxed. Packed one gross per carton in assorted colours. 7/- per dozen.
Retail 1/-

**1162 D Dalek Bagatelle**
Upright design. 9" high and 10" wide. Individually boxed. Packed one dozen per carton. 51/8 per dozen.
Retail 7/6

**SUPER TOYS BY MARX**

That was a shame. They weren't the models they could have been... There was a Dalek suit made out of PVC with a load of hoops and it was about as realistic and frightening as a jelly bag. They didn't contain that fear, that mechanised quality that children love to be frightened by.'

Richard has a point, of course – the shape had been simplified when the Daleks entered mass production, resulting in toys which looked more conical than the TV Daleks; it would be another forty years before the *Doctor Who* production office ensured that Dalek toys matched up to the real thing. But the 1960s toys were incredibly popular, and thousands of children grew up with very happy memories of commanding their own Dalek armies.

Some of those Dalek toys even found their way into *Doctor Who* itself in the 1960s and 1970s, standing in for full-size taskforces and armies in *The Power of the Daleks*, *The Evil of the Daleks* and *Planet of the Daleks*.

# Doctor Who and the Daleks

Ten weeks before the Dalek comic strip began in *TV Century 21*, the long-running *TV Comic* had introduced its own *Doctor Who* strip. Unable to secure the rights to the Daleks, *TV Comic*'s Doctor Who and his grandchildren John and Gillian were forced to battle the Trods, a race of conical robots from the planet Trodos who ran on static electricity and built their own time machine in order to hunt down the *Tardis*...

Two years later, the rights to use the Daleks in comic strips passed to *TV Comic*. The final *TVC21* Dalek strip appeared on 13 January 1967 and, eight days later, Doctor Who, John and Gillian arrived on Trodos to find that the Daleks had invaded – massacring the Trods – and were now firmly established. *TV Comic*'s strip was renamed *Doctor Who and the Daleks* and, for the next few months, Doctor Who couldn't land on an alien planet to test his new explorer truck or pedal copter without running into the dastardly Daleks.

After 22 issues, the Daleks abruptly vanished from both the comic strip and its title. Just as *TV Comic*'s Doctor was trying to prevent a mad scientist giving zoo animals an obedience drug while reviving dinosaurs in New York, BBC One's Doctor was watching the Dalek city burn and declaring the Daleks' 'final end'...

## DALEKS – INVASION USA 1967 AD

*The Evil of the Daleks* was intended to be the Daleks' final appearance in *Doctor Who*. Terry Nation, who – as their creator – owned the characters, had been trying for a couple of years to drum up interest in the Daleks as the possible stars of their own TV series in the USA. By late 1966, Nation had drafted an opening story, and it seemed likely that *The Daleks* would enter production and begin transmission within a year. Ultimately, though, legal difficulties and protracted negotiations meant that *The Daleks* would never be made.

Terry Nation's draft script for *The Destroyers* drew on the fictional worlds that Nation had created, not only in *Doctor Who* but also in the various licensed books and comic strips over which he had exercised creative control. The storyline features SSS Agent Sara Kingdom, originally created for the 1965–1966 television story *The Daleks' Master Plan*, alongside another agent, Jason Corey, and an android Mark 7, both derived from characters devised for *The Dalek Outer Space Book* (1966). Attempting to locate Sara's missing brother, David Kingdom, the three SSS agents discover a Dalek plan to attack and annihilate planet Earth. As the episode concludes, the Daleks are initiating Phase Two of their plan, with subsequent episodes clearly intended to show Sara and co's attempts to prevent Dalek domination of the galaxy.

Very little was known about this aborted spin-off until 2009, when TV historian Andrew Pixley revealed its history in *Doctor Who Magazine*. Terry Nation's script survives and was recorded as an audio play by Big Finish in 2010, with actor Jean Marsh returning to the role of Sara Kingdom.

# Temporal Power

Held prisoner in the Dalek city on Skaro, the First Doctor told the Daleks he had a ship that could travel through space and time:

> **FIRST DALEK**
> Now that we know of the machine, we can examine it for ourselves.
>
> **DOCTOR**
> But you can't operate it without me!
>
> **FIRST DALEK**
> Every problem has a solution.

**THE DALEKS**
by Terry Nation

Having learned that time travel was a theoretical possibility, the Daleks set about making it a reality. By the time their invasion of Earth was defeated they had the ability to track the TARDIS through time and space. Their prototype time machine was a dimensionally transcendental box, which accurately followed the Doctor to various locations, although he thought it was a very unreliable piece of technology. In the year 4000, the Daleks were still using the same timeships, which were kept on Skaro and used only by specially trained taskforces for specific missions.

The evolution of time-corridor technology prompted a new tactic: the Daleks would rule in the present by conquering the past. The Daleks stabilised a corridor linking Skaro in the far future with an English house in 1866. Daleks were able to move freely between Earth in 1866 and 1966 and Skaro in the far future. Though the Dalek Factor plan backfired, the Emperor's stratagem of pre-conquering the universe survived the Civil War, and time corridors were used to despatch taskforces back in time to reverse earlier setbacks, such as the defeated invasion of Earth. This set up unstable new timelines, built on paradoxes.

The Daleks refined the technology, and were eventually able to construct links from deep space in the 46th century back to 1980s London and out to far-flung colony worlds in the distant future. It was also a form of time scoop, able to capture the Doctor's TARDIS. Individual Daleks and even entire battle fleets could be moved through the time corridors.

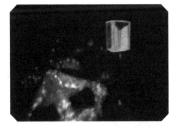

# YEARS OF DOOM

**DAY OF THE DALEKS**
**by Louis Marks**
Starring Jon Pertwee
as the Doctor
**First broadcast:**
01/01/1972–22/01/1972

The humanised Daleks were eventually defeated and, in the aftermath of the Civil War, the survivors of the Dalek race began to rebuild. A new hierarchy was established: the Black Daleks were now replaced by a new gold-coloured Commander rank, and a Supreme Council was formed, led by the Dalek Supreme. Most importantly, the Daleks effected a rare series of improvements on themselves. The new generation finally overcame the need for a means of drawing power from external sources – they now moved independently by psychokinetic power. They had also incorporated an automatic distress call into the communications system that linked them all; the alarm was triggered whenever a Dalek was attacked.

With his Dalek Factor plan, the Emperor had established the principle that the whole of history could be altered to achieve a Dalek victory. Time-corridor technology was now used to shift Dalek forces into the past. It is even possible that this was a daring scheme to transport the entirety of surviving Dalek civilisation back to an earlier era, re-conquer Skaro and begin to undo past defeats before they occurred. One fleet attacked Earth almost two centuries before the failed Project De-Gravitate. They wiped out seven-eighths of the population and enslaved the rest, using subservient

**TRACKING DALEK TIMELINES**

41st century ➤➤ Dalek Civil War ➤➤ 41st century
41st century ➤➤ Timeship flees Skaro and crashes on
Vulcan ➤➤ 21st century
20th century ➤➤ The Dalek invasion of Earth v2
➤➤ 22nd century

This was the Third Doctor's first encounter with the Daleks, who failed to recognise him and were able to confirm his identity only by using a mind probe. Details of their enemy's new guise were transmitted to Supreme Command, and the new generation of Daleks were only too aware of him at their next confrontation...

humans as Controllers and the Ogrons as a brutal police force. The Daleks then began the thorough mineral exploitation of Earth, to gain the natural resources to build a new Dalek army.

But the new invasion, overwriting the later one, was based on a temporal paradox. It had been made possible by a world war that had fatally weakened the human race in the late 20th century. That war had been provoked by the bombing of a peace conference by a time-travelling guerrilla from the 22nd century – and he had travelled back in time in the belief that his actions would prevent the Dalek invasion. Instead, his act had opened the way to the conquest. This timeline's Dalek invasion and its underlying paradox were undone by the Doctor, now in his third body and exiled to 20th-century Earth by the Time Lords.

# The Ogrons

Depleted Dalek numbers in the aftermath of the Civil War forced the Supreme Council to use other races to back up their invasions. The Ogrons were used as a thuggish police force in the restaged invasion of Earth, helping the collaborating human Controllers to keep the populace subdued and productive. The Master and the Daleks later used them as part of their attempts to provoke a war between Earth and Draconia.

The Ogrons are an ape-like race who make very obedient servants. Extremely tall and exceptionally strong, they are also simple-minded, vicious and loyal. They are easily intimidated by those they serve – terrified by the mere sight of a Dalek or of their 'god' (an amorphous predator on their home world).

# The Controlled and the Controllers

▶▶ **ARTHUR TERRALL:** A guest in Maxtible's household in 1866, Terrall was controlled by a more advanced version of the conditioning process used on the Robomen. He received Dalek commands via a small device in his clothing, which generated an electromagnetic field around his body. The conditioning was not total – he was still capable of independent thought and action, and seemed frequently unaware that he was under the power of the Daleks, acting against their instructions during periods of free will. The side effects of the process caused him great pain. The processing was unreliable and easily reversed.

▶▶ **THE CONTROLLERS:** When the Doctor and Jo Grant were transported to the 22nd century, they saw what Earth would be like after 200 years of Dalek rule. The invading Daleks had left only a small taskforce to run the planet. As well as the Ogrons, the Daleks relied on a Controller, a human collaborator who directed operations from a site fifty miles north of London, probably in Bedfordshire. Planetary administration was monitored by seemingly emotionless, identically attired female servants. When addressing these assistants, the Controller issued commands in a flat, Dalek-like monotone, and was answered similarly. It is not known whether his assistants were processed or were deliberately suppressing any emotional expression or individuality.

The first Controller was selected from among the survivors of the invasion. His role was to oversee mining operations and ensure production levels fulfilled Dalek quotas. Commanding an elite of human guards, as well as the Ogrons, he could order the punishment, torture or death of resistance fighters and traitors, and any slaves who failed to meet their targets. The position became hereditary: the Controller encountered by the Doctor and Jo was the third in his family to inherit the title. He lived under the constant threat of punishment and extermination. Inspired by the Doctor, he eventually rebelled against the Daleks and was exterminated.

# Perhaps They Just Enjoy Subjugating Humanoid Races

Daleks don't just exterminate, they also humiliate. They have always understood that the most effective way of subjugating a population is to set it against itself, and a constant feature of their conquests is the degradation of the civilian population, who are forced into almost totally pointless manual labour.

Project De-Gravitate saw the Daleks turn the whole of Bedfordshire into a labour camp. They used advanced mining machinery to drill down to the Earth's core, but clearing the debris was the task of slave workforces. The slaves were starved, and beaten by their own robotised relatives. The work seemingly achieved very little, beyond providing a useful source of hostages. But it was part of a pattern that the Daleks would follow for thousands of years, from Aridius and Spiridon to Exxilon and the Medusa Cascade. When the Daleks travelled back in time to reinvade the Earth they established similar labour camps. Two centuries of control over the Earth showed how an entire planet could be run by limited Dalek forces. As well as using their Ogron mercenaries, the Daleks turned humanity against itself, through the use of Controllers.

The Daleks often form temporary alliances at gunpoint. More cunningly, the Daleks enslave people through their own weaknesses. This is frequently greed: Mavic Chen was promised power, Lesterson was tempted by the acclaim of scientific discovery, and Maxtible was offered the secret of alchemy.

> **MAXTIBLE**
> I have done everything you have asked me to. You wanted an agency here on Earth to plan and prepare things for you. I have been that agency. Will you please tell those who give you orders that I am getting tired of waiting.
>
> **DALEK**
> Do you threaten the Daleks?
>
> **MAXTIBLE**
> Oh, surely threatening is not necessary. We have a.. a partnership - an understanding.
>
> **DALEK**
> You have obeyed us.
>
> **MAXTIBLE**
> You have a strange way of putting things. I prefer to say that you have asked for certain services. I have provided those services punctually and efficiently. Now you really must look to your side of the bargain. It is not beyond me to ruin the entire enterprise.
>
> (The DALEK attacks Maxtible.)
>
> **THE EVIL OF THE DALEKS**
> by David Whitaker

## DALEKMANIA

### Countdown

Within a couple of episodes of their return to *Doctor Who* on television in *Day of the Daleks*, the Daleks had also rematerialised in the *Doctor Who* comic strip. By this time, the strip had moved from *TV Comic* to a new home: *Countdown for TV Action!* The magazine was targeted at a slightly older audience than *TV Comic*, as shown by the Daleks' first appearance. In 'Sub Zero', they destroy Sydney from a nuclear submarine and convert the survivors into Daleks. This eight-part adventure was immediately followed by an eight-part return to Skaro – 'The Planet of the Daleks' – in which the Doctor is apparently infected with the Dalek Factor and becomes the new Dalek leader. A year later, the renamed *TV Action* presented 'The Threat from Beneath', which sees the Daleks taking control of another nuclear submarine.

Towards the end of 1973, *TV Action* was absorbed into *TV Comic*, where the *Doctor Who* strip continued. A further Dalek appearance was scheduled to coincide with *Death to the Daleks* in early 1974. 'The Disintegrator' begins with the Doctor investigating a bank robbery, which turns out to be the work of the Daleks; the five-part story concludes on the moon, where a neutron bomb is turned against the Daleks.

### 'We Are the Daleks!'

To mark the series' 10th anniversary in November 1973, *Radio Times* published a commemorative *Doctor Who* special. The magazine included detailed plans for building a life-sized Dalek and some new fiction – a short story written by Terry Nation.

A year later, Nation would unveil Davros as the Dalek creator. A decade earlier, the *TVC21* comic strip had shown Yarvelling inventing the Daleks. Now 'We Are the Daleks!' offered a very different account of Dalek origins: scientists from the planet Halldon capture primitive humans and take them to the planet Ameron, where their evolution is accelerated, and they become the first Daleks.

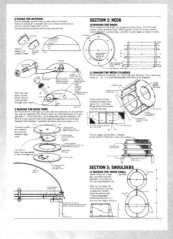

# DESTINATION: DALEKS

The new generation of post-Civil War Daleks abandoned the ruins of Skaro and once more swarmed across the galaxies. Did they fulfil the ultimate logic of the Emperor's plans for gaining supremacy by temporal manipulation? This might have meant overwriting their race's own timeline, restaging past battles, perhaps even exterminating their own earlier selves. Or were the Daleks that menaced Draconia and Earth in the 26th century *always* from millennia into the future? Were there, in fact, two types of Dalek from different eras, co-existing throughout this time? With the Daleks so reckless with their own and other races' timelines, it is impossible to be certain. Not least because the Doctor wasn't the only Time Lord caught up in Dalek affairs during this era of Dalek history. The Master, too, became involved with the Daleks.

**FRONTIER IN SPACE**
**by Malcolm Hulke**
Starring Jon Pertwee as the Doctor
**First broadcast:**
24/02/1973–31/03/1973

To prevent the Earth and Draconian empires of the 26th century joining forces to repel the Dalek attack on their galaxy (see Space Wars, p.35), the Master invented a gadget that induced Earthmen to see Ogrons as Draconians, and Draconians to see them as Earthmen. Ogron spaceships raided cargo freighters from both empires, sparking a series of diplomatic incidents. When the TARDIS landed on an Earth cargo ship in the year 2540 in time to witness an Ogron raid, the situation had already escalated to the brink of war. The Doctor eventually persuaded the governments of Earth and Draconia that the provocations were the work of a third party, then tracked the Master to the Ogrons' home world. Only when he was ambushed by the Master and a Dalek taskforce – led by one of the new gold-coloured Dalek Commanders – did the Doctor realise that the Master's scheme was designed to weaken and divide Earth and Draconia in preparation for a sustained Dalek assault.

## TRACKING DALEK TIMELINES

20th century ▶▶ The Dalek invasion of Earth v2 ▶▶ 22nd century 2540 ▶▶ Ogron raids on Earth/Draconia ▶▶ 2540 2540 ▶▶ Dalek army sealed on Spiridon ▶▶ 2540

The Daleks encountered by the Doctor on the Ogron world and on Spiridon were from a time far beyond the 26th century – not only did they now recognise his third form, but their own appearance and command structure were those of the new generation of Daleks that arose on Skaro in the aftermath of the Civil War.

**PLANET OF THE DALEKS**
by Terry Nation
Starring Jon Pertwee as the Doctor
**First broadcast:** 07/04/1973–12/05/1973

The Master's plan failed, but the Daleks continued with their real project: building a new Dalek army, concealed on the planet Spiridon. The Doctor appealed to the Time Lords for help locating the Daleks. They sent him to Spiridon, where a Dalek scientific taskforce was attempting to discover the secret of the inhabitants' natural invisibility. The new generation of Daleks clearly understood that the most certain route to domination was by stealth. However, a squad of Thals from Skaro joined forces with the Doctor to entomb the Dalek army in Spiridon's underground ice caverns, and the Dalek scientists were killed by their own experimental bacteria bomb. When the Doctor was identified, the Dalek Supreme headed for Spiridon, arriving in time to witness the ruination of Dalek plans. The Supreme was stranded on the jungle world when the Thals made off in its spacecraft.

These setbacks severely weakened the Daleks, who were unable to gain the upper hand in the Dalek Wars that followed. Earth and Draconia united to combat the Dalek threat and, once again, the Daleks turned to germ warfare.

## Draconians

The Draconians were a race of cultured reptilian aliens with an advanced civilisation. Their society was tradition-bound along strict hierarchical lines, with all Draconians owing fealty to their Emperor, and females being forbidden to speak in his presence. Earth and Draconia fought a brief and terrible space war in the early 26th century before maintaining an uneasy peace for two decades. The truce was threatened by the intervention of the Master, working for the Daleks. Although the Draconians had not at that time met the Daleks, they would later join an unusual alliance with them...

# Spiridon

A planet in the Ninth System, Spiridon was interesting to the Daleks for several reasons – the plant life of its jungles was deadly, its dominant species was invisible, and its core was molten ice. Its climate was tropical by day but extremely cold at night. Its natural features included molten ice pools caused by the random eruptions of ice volcanoes, and the Plain of Stones – large boulders which absorbed and stored the warmth of Spiridon's sun.

The planet's flora gave the appearance of semi-sentience: tentacle-like growths would lunge for animal life forms; eyeplants tracked movement, providing an indication of approaching danger; and fungus plants spat a toxic infection that spread across animal flesh, consuming it. Yet the jungle vegetation also supplied an antidote to that fungoid infection.

Although naturally invisible, the Spiridons wore purple animal furs to protect themselves against the cold. The Spiridons became visible after death, appearing humanoid. They had constructed a city on the outskirts of the jungle, built into the sides of an ice volcano, which provided a natural cooling system for the city. When the Daleks invaded, they converted the city for their own use and built a huge refrigeration unit in its lower levels.

# DALEK HIERARCHY

## The Dalek Supreme

After the Civil War, a Supreme Council was established, with the Dalek Supreme at its head. Its gold and black-coloured casing had a number of differences from the standard Dalek shell, including a more substantial eyepiece, which flashed in the same rhythm as its – also larger – dome lights. It supervised Dalek operations from its Command Spacecraft, occasionally travelling to sites of significant Dalek activity such as Spiridon.

## Commanders

The Black Dalek tier, from which Saucer Commanders and Dalek Supremes had been drawn until the Civil War, was now replaced by the general Commander rank. These Commanders were distinguished by their gold-coloured casings. They controlled individual taskforces and spacecraft, and reported to the Supreme Council.

## Dalek Leaders

Smaller taskforces like the scientific group based on Spiridon were led by standard drone Daleks designated Dalek Leaders. They reported to the gold Commanders and, ultimately, to the Supreme Council and the Dalek Supreme, and were held accountable for any failures – the Dalek Leader on Spiridon was exterminated after the Doctor, the Thals and rebel Spiridons successfully sabotaged the Dalek mission.

## 'It's the Daleks!'

 'Do not move! Do not move! Do not move! Do not move! Do not move! Do not move! You are our prisoner! Do not move! You are our prisoner!'

'When I give the word, turn and dive into the water ... Now!'

'Get down, get down!' 'Oh! What's the matter?' 'Keep your head down.'

'What's this?' 'A liquid colour spray.' 'Point it in this direction, press the control on top and you'll see what we're up against.' 'Daleks!'

'Come on out. The welcome party's all here!' 'Daleks!' 'The Earth creatures are to be exterminated! Fire at my command!'

# THE EXXILONS

**DEATH TO THE DALEKS**
by Terry Nation
Starring Jon Pertwee
as the Doctor
**First broadcast:**
23/02/1974–16/03/1974

Beaten back in the Wars, the Daleks began to bombard Earth's outer colony worlds with bacteria bombs, spreading a virulent plague. The only known cure was parrinium, and Earth's empire despatched countless ships in search of planets rich in the mineral. The Daleks were doing the same – or perhaps even simply waiting for an Earth team to identify a parrinium-rich world then following them.

One such planet was Exxilon, a barren world dominated by a huge, sentient city. The city itself had drained most of Exxilon's resources,

sending its inhabitants backwards into primitivism and superstition, and was able to drain power from passing interstellar vessels. The Earth survey team sent to Exxilon found the parrinium source they needed, but were unable to escape the planet, while the Dalek taskforce that followed

them there found themselves similarly short of power. Ever innovative, the Daleks simply exchanged their defunct ray-gun attachments for projectile weapons and set about the conquest of Exxilon. Yet again, their plans were thwarted by the presence of the Doctor and the ingenuity and bravery of Earth personnel. With the city disabled and dying, the Dalek scoutship took off from Exxilon, planning to bombard the planet's surface with bacteria bombs. But, thanks to the Doctor's companion, Sarah Jane Smith, the ship's cargo holds contained sacks of sand not parrinium – plus one human. Dan Galloway stowed away armed with a Dalek bomb, with which he blew up the Dalek craft.

The havoc of the Dalek Wars continued into the 27th century and beyond. Meanwhile, another power began to pay attention to Dalek activity. The Time Lords of Gallifrey had simply observed as the Daleks began their original wave of conquests and had not intervened, even when they developed time-travel technology. The combination, however, of the Daleks' large-scale efforts to alter history, the Master's alliance with them and the Doctor's subsequent appeal for help seems to have motivated the Time Lords to take a closer look. They now foretold a time when the Daleks would achieve their aim and destroy all other life forms in the cosmos. This was a future the Time Lords could not allow to happen…

### TRACKING DALEK TIMELINES
2540 ⏵⏵ Dalek army sealed on Spiridon ⏵⏵ 2540
2540 ⏵⏵ The Dalek Wars ⏵⏵ 3000
c.2600 ⏵⏵ The Exxilon mission ⏵⏵ c.2600

The Dalek taskforce on Exxilon had clearly suffered the privations of the long-drawn-out Dalek Wars of the preceding decades. Their appearance suggests that this taskforce may have been from the Daleks' original timestream, now subsumed into the prevailing new Dalek forces.

## WE HAVE CHANGED THE PATTERN OF HISTORY!

## Exxilons

The Exxilons were once a great race of explorers – they travelled the galaxy, influencing many developing cultures before building a great city on their home world. The ultimate expression of their civilisation, it was self-sustaining and autonomous – and drove out its creators. Some hid underground and retained the vestiges of culture, whereas those who survived on the planet's surface descended into savagery, worshipping the city as a god and offering sacrifices to it.

## DALEKMANIA

### Seven Keys to Doomsday

Between Jon Pertwee's last regular appearance as the Third Doctor and the beginning of Tom Baker's reign as the Fourth, a second *Doctor Who* play was produced on the London stage. *Doctor Who and the Daleks in Seven Keys to Doomsday* ran at the Adelphi Theatre for four weeks from 16 December 1974. Accompanied by two plucky assistants who were planted in the audience, the Doctor regenerated into actor Trevor Martin before battling to prevent the Daleks from conquering the universe.

Written by Terrance Dicks, the story involves the Doctor and the Daleks in a race to uncover the seven components of an all-powerful crystal. The Daleks are aided by the Clawrentulars, an enslaved species of giant crabs, and later scenes revive the Dalek Emperor last seen in *The Evil of the Daleks*.

Terrance Dicks later adapted his script for

Big Finish Productions, whose audio version was released in 2008, again starring Trevor Martin as the Doctor.

# WE FORESEE A TIME...

T he Time Lords sent the Doctor to Skaro in the dying days of the thousand-year war. His mission was to prevent the creation of the Daleks or, at the very least, to alter their development so that they would evolve into less aggressive creatures. When he left Skaro some time later, the Doctor suggested that he might have set the Daleks back a thousand years or so, but this seems to have been more hope than reality. The Doctor's mere presence had unintended consequences...

**GENESIS OF THE DALEKS**
by Terry Nation
Starring Tom Baker as the Doctor
**First broadcast:**
08/03/1975–12/04/1975

The travel-machine project was very advanced, but had significantly changed direction as Davros sought to turn his creations into a weapon. He had devised a way to accelerate the Kaled race's mutation and had already built up a store of mutant embryos. The Mark III travel machines were functioning effectively, with accurate and deadly weaponry, although improvements were needed in the optical systems and sensory circuits. Davros had established voice control over the mutated creatures once they were installed in the machines, and they were also capable of autonomous action. Through genetic manipulation, Davros was creating machine creatures with an in-bred hatred for all non-conformity.

Those among the Kaled Scientific Elite already troubled by the direction of Davros's research found new hope after the Doctor's arrival. Senior Researcher Ronson, until now unable even to contact the Kaled city, risked his life to help the

Doctor and Harry escape the Bunker and address the Kaled government. A persuasive speech from the Doctor prompted the councillors to move against Davros, who was informed that all ongoing projects would be suspended and investigated. Davros saw this interference as justification for the sacrifice of the whole of the Kaled people. He ordered the installation of twenty mutant embryos in the Dalek machines, knowing that they were erratic and unstable but intending to write a computer program limiting the extent of their self-control. He then betrayed his race, giving the Thals the chemical formula that allowed their rocket to penetrate the Kaled dome and destroy the city beneath it.

Davros now turned his attention to the Doctor. Computer analysis of his blood and chemical make-up confirmed that his physiological composition conformed to no known life form on Skaro. Davros had concluded that Skaro was the only planet in the seven known galaxies capable of supporting intelligent life. The Doctor's presence proved him wrong, and Davros quickly recognised that his Daleks must have a far greater destiny than he had imagined, since aliens from the future were interfering at their birth. His ambition for his creations had previously been limited to the conquest of Skaro and the annihilation of the Thals. Now he saw the Daleks not simply as a weapon to win the war, but as a species capable of ruling the universe. He quickly developed new ways to power the machines, freeing them from their dependence on static electricity so they could venture beyond the metal walkways of the Bunker and the surrounding network of tunnels. Their first mission saw them traverse the wastelands of Skaro to attack the Thal city – at a stroke one of the Daleks' earliest limitations had been removed from their history.

Davros, meanwhile, stepped up the genetic restructuring of the mutant embryos, reasoning that if his Daleks were to survive, they must ruthlessly suppress all other life forms. He introduced a new set of chromosomal variations to remove conscience, morality, feeling and emotion in their entirety. He also intended to continue adjusting and improving the travel machines – for Davros, the Daleks remained an ongoing and far from perfect project. He did not complete it.

Whether Davros omitted to write the computer program limiting Dalek actions, or whether that program was simply inadequate to overcome the prototype Daleks' aggression and instability is unknown. Davros's creations turned on him. They exterminated the remaining Kaled Elite, then fired on Davros himself. For a short time after the Doctor left Skaro, the Daleks were sealed in the Bunker, but it is unlikely they were contained for long. They were already planning a campaign of universal conquest. The Daleks' future history would now be very different...

**TRACKING DALEK TIMELINES**

c.450 ▶▶ The thousand-year war ▶▶ c.1450

c.1450 ▶▶ The (re-)creation of the Daleks ▶▶ c.1450

**New timeline established**

## Defeats Will Become Victories

With his friends Sarah Jane Smith and Harry Sullivan being tortured in front of him, the Doctor revealed the Daleks' future history to Davros...

▶▶ The Dalek invasion of the planet Earth in the year 2000 was foiled because of the attempt by the Daleks to mine the magnetic core of the planet. The magnetic properties of the Earth were too powerful.

▶▶ On Mars, the Daleks were defeated by a virus that attacked the insulation on cables in their electrical systems.

▶▶ The Dalek war against the Venusians in the space year 17000 was ended by the intervention of a fleet of war rockets from the planet Hyperon. The rockets were made from a metal that was completely resistant to Dalek firepower, and the Dalek taskforce was completely destroyed.

**NB:** *The Doctor was attached to highly sensitive equipment that would detect any attempt to lie; however, the sensors were not calibrated to react to his erratic memory.*

# Davros

Davros was born during the final century of the Kaled-Thal war – his earliest memory was of hiding in bomb shelters, deep underground, hearing the screams of battle on the planet's surface. His extraordinary intelligence and scientific aptitude were evident from an early age; it was inevitable that he would end up leading the Kaled Elite Scientific Corps.

As a young man, Davros was caught in an explosion while working in his laboratory. He was rescued from the rubble, his legs useless, one arm smashed and beyond repair, his sight and hearing damaged, his organs failing, his now hairless scalp blistered and peeling. Determined to survive, he designed a complete life-support system, building the remains of his body into a mobile chair, from which his head, torso and remaining withered hand and arm emerged, all supported by a harness. His body and skull were wired into the chair's systems, allowing him to control its basic movements psychokinetically. The chair also contained electro-mechanical substitutes for his failed heart and lungs, while a network of tubes kept up a constant stream of chemical nutrients, removing any need to eat or drink. He replaced his ruined sight with an electronic scanner, its single lens wired into his forehead, and implanted an incredibly sensitive audio system in place of his lost hearing. His vocal cords, too, were damaged, so

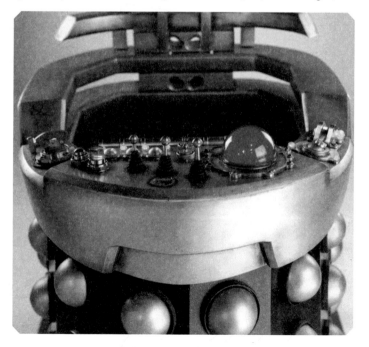

he installed a tiny vocaliser, with a throat-mounted microphone creating and amplifying an electronically enhanced voice. Over the next few decades, he continued to modify and adapt the chair, even developing a circuit that fed impulses into his brain to negate the urge to sleep. He built in failsafe procedures enabling the long-term suspension of his bodily organs and an automatic process of synthetic tissue regeneration.

At the front of the chair was a board of controls and switches and hidden compartments, which he was constantly adding to, allowing him to remote-operate doors, computer and communications equipment, even prototype Daleks. The most important of these were linked directly to his life-support systems. Though Davros refused to permit himself 'the luxury of death', a part of him still yearned for it, and he fitted a control switch with which he could suspend the whole system. But he also put in a secondary life-support system, wary of his death being brought about by anyone or anything other than himself.

## CREATING DAVROS

Actor Michael Wisher was cast as Davros by director David Maloney. Wisher had provided Dalek voices for three of their encounters with Jon Pertwee's Doctor and had taken roles in another three Third Doctor serials. Knowing that he would spend six episodes sitting in a chair and wearing a close-fitting mask that would restrict his vision and hearing, Wisher prepared himself for the part by rehearsing with a paper bag over his head. To achieve a voice suggestive of the Daleks, Wisher's lines were fed through a ring modulator.

Visual effects sculptor John Friedlander modelled the mask around Wisher's face. It was made of latex, and entirely covered the actor's head, exposing only his mouth – Wisher's teeth and tongue were blackened to add to the impression of physical deterioration. The Davros chair was built by designer Peter Day and the BBC Visual Effects department and was based on the lower half of a Dalek prop.

# DALEKMANIA

## Return of the Daleks!

The first broadcast of *Genesis of the Daleks* in February 1975 enabled *TV Comic* to continue its traditional spring return of the Daleks, with 'Return of the Daleks!' This was the Fourth Doctor's second comic-strip adventure, an eight-part epic with the Daleks working alongside a renegade half-Time Lord called Shazar. The Time Lords are shown on their home world (named Jewel not Gallifrey). The Daleks manage to construct their own fleet of TARDISes, but this is destroyed when they use incompatible fuel rods.

Almost a year later, 'The Dalek Revenge' consisted of taking over the planet Ercos and converting it into a missile large enough to destroy Earth, a plan quite consistent with the TV Daleks' own schemes, such as Project De-Gravitate. In the process they round up a slave workforce for a huge mining operation, and enlist an ally from among their slaves, a traitor whom they subsequently exterminate.

The *Doctor Who* strip ran for another three years, increasingly relying on reprints of older stories adapted for Tom Baker's Doctor.

But aside from a strip titled 'Invasion' – actually a (fourth) doctored reprint of the Third Doctor strip 'The Threat from Beneath' – that was it for the Daleks in *TV Comic*.

## 'What Are Your Orders?'

The ever-increasing popularity of *Doctor Who* during the Jon Pertwee and Tom Baker eras prompted a new wave of tie-in merchandising in the mid 1970s, which inevitably centred on the Doctor's battles with the Daleks. There were iron-on transfers and painting-by-numbers sets, and a 'Doctor Who and the Daleks Yo-Yo', while a board game called 'War of the Daleks' challenged up to four players to evade patrolling Daleks and reach the centre of the game board, thus destroying the Dalek Emperor. A leading breakfast cereal even gave away sets of colour stand-up figures of the Doctor, his companions and his enemies, including half a dozen different Daleks, with the backs of the cereal packets providing 'action settings' for their cardboard adventures. In 1976, it was the turn of tea-

drinkers to use enough teabags to accumulate a dozen collector's cards, Davros and a Dalek among them. The following year, fans of wheat biscuits were treated to more stand-up figures with their breakfasts, this time including Davros and the Daleks, and even advertised on 'the other side' (ITV) – an excitable red Dalek addressed the camera to strongly recommend collecting the whole set and eating a lot of wheat.

Probably the most sought-after new item was issued in 1975 by Palitoy Bradgate – a 16 cm silver or red plastic Talking Dalek. A button on the dome activated one of four Dalek

Computer which can accurately tell you which day of the week any date fell on up to the year 2000, and Mark 7 shattered all existing records at the Robotic Olympic Games.

The *Dalek Annual 1978* includes a biography of Davros, which provides extensive details of the changes he made to his own body to prolong his life and explanations of the controls and functions of his chair. The article concludes: 'The dead body of Davros is buried somewhere beneath the millions of tons of rubble that caved in from the roof of his workshops. Or is it? There is a legend that people tell in space. It is said that Davros had built into his life support system a device that would keep him in a condition of suspended animation; that the spark of life could never die. Some people believe that if his body is ever recovered he could again be brought to full and active life.' It was published in September 1977, two years before Davros's televised return in *Destiny of the Daleks* – a return Terry Nation was obviously already contemplating...

exclamations: ▶▶ Attack! Attack! Attack! ▶▶ What are your orders? ▶▶ I will obey! ▶▶ Exterminate! Exterminate!

A couple of years later, Denys Fisher Toys released a set of six *Doctor Who* action figures, around 24 cm high, including a fairly accurate Dalek. The toy had the silver and blue colour scheme of the 1960s Daleks, topped with a red dome.

## Terry Nation's Dalek Annual

Between 1975 and 1978, World Distributors published a *Dalek Annual* each September. These comprised reprints from the *TVC21* comics alongside new stories about the Anti-Dalek Force founded by the Galactic President Cal Tarrant, and the adventures of the Dalek-fighting android Mark 7.

A series of supporting features divulged facts about the Daleks and their opponents – ADF headquarters, for example, contains a vast Time

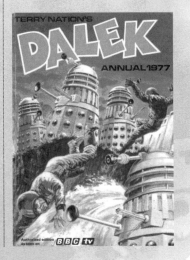

# STALEMATE

DESTINY OF
THE DALEKS
**by Terry Nation**
Starring Tom Baker as
the Doctor
**First broadcast:**
01/09/1979–22/09/1979

The peoples of the universe have long seen the Dalek as the ultimate terror – a ruthless killing machine, entirely devoid of feelings and compassion, its reasoning coldly logical, its purpose subjugation and extermination. The Daleks that emerged from the Kaled bunker in the wake of the Doctor's intervention were, if anything, more Dalek than the Daleks had ever been before. There are no records to indicate to what extent Dalek history over the next two or three millennia differed from the events of their previous timeline. When the Fourth Doctor returned to Skaro in the early 46th century, the ruins of the Kaled city were still standing, suggesting that in this new timeline the Daleks had not constructed Kalaann over its remains. There was also no sign of any Thals, and Skaro's air was still saturated with radiation – the neutron war that followed the Daleks' creation must have been even more devastating than in the original timeline.

Perhaps the Doctor was correct – he'd set the Daleks back a thousand years, and Earth was not now invaded until 3157, for example. Or, possibly, their history was played out more or less the same. This subtly different version of the Daleks was more brutal and effective, but these Daleks did not have the innate cunning of the race

**TRACKING DALEK TIMELINES**
c.1450 >> The (re-)creation of the Daleks >> c.1450
**New timeline established**
42nd century >> The Dalek-Movellan
war >> 46th century
4500 >> The Daleks resurrect Davros >> 4500

that earlier Doctors had met. The organic element of the Dalek creatures became increasingly marginalised – and, as far as a Dalek could be said to pretend, they were pretending very hard to be creatures of pure logic. The Daleks really had become machine creatures, ruled by logical certainties. In their original timeline they recognised and exploited qualities like pity and compassion in other species. Now they simply had no understanding of the concepts, the words not even registered in their vocabulary banks.

Their brains were effectively computerised. They were no longer the scarred survivors of the Kaled race but were instead imitations of robotic automata. So when the Daleks came up against an actual race of ruthlessly logical robotic automata – the Movellans – the result was neither victory nor defeat.

Some three thousand years after they had attempted to execute him, the Daleks returned to Skaro in search of Davros. With each Dalek equipped to scan for and detect life signs, the Daleks must have realised that Davros was not dead, yet they had chosen to leave him entombed in their city, a discarded relic from their past. Now, however, they needed

him, and they dug deep into their heritage to locate him.

A Movellan taskforce followed the Daleks to Skaro, its mission to discover the Dalek plan and halt it. When the Doctor explained what the Daleks were up to, however, the Movellans quickly adapted, reasoning that the Doctor could give them the same advantage over the Daleks as Davros offered his creations. Instead, the Doctor led an insurgency by the Daleks' human slaves. The Movellan and Dalek squads were both destroyed, and Davros was placed in cryogenic suspension pending his trial by Earth authorities.

# Movellans

The Movellans came from star system 4X Alpha 4. Outwardly beautiful humanoids in appearance, they were careful to preserve the secret that they were actually a race of androids – although they could create a reasonable approximation of emotion and facial expressions, they were actually completely logical. Despite this, they had names, personalities and ranks, and even fitted out their spaceships with soft furnishings – to preserve the illusion, or because their programming demanded they try to be as humanoid as possible.

The outward clues to their true robotic nature were their preternatural calm in extreme circumstances and their massive strength. Careful observers might also note that apparently deceased Movellans would soon be seen alive and well again, and that they depended on an externally fitted power pack, which also relayed their instructions.

**DAVROS**
A concise report and a fascinating problem. The Daleks have met a foe worthy of their powers. Another race of robots.

**DALEK**
Correct. Dalek superiority will ultimately triumph and the Movellan force will be exterminated.

**DAVROS**
You have been fighting them for centuries, and still you are not victorious!

**DALEK**
It is only a matter of time.

**DAVROS**
No. Two gigantic computerised battle fleets locked together in deep space, hundreds of galactic battle cruisers vying with each other for centuries, and not a shot fired?

**DALEK**
Our computers are planning the moment of maximum advantage.

**DAVROS**
And so are theirs. It will never come. You have reached a logical impasse.

**DALEK**
Understood.

**DAVROS**
So that is why you have returned to find your creator.

**DALEK**
You will reprogram our battle computers for us. The Movellans will be exterminated!

**DESTINY OF THE DALEKS**
by Terry Nation

When they encountered the Daleks, both races were evenly matched and their battle computers soon reached a stalemate – their fleets suspended in space unable to fire a shot as each side predicted every manoeuvre. This situation endured for centuries, until the showdown on Skaro. Following the Daleks' failure to secure Davros, however, the Movellans eventually triumphed, winning the war by developing a virus lethal to their enemies, and reducing Dalek forces to a few scattered survivors.

Yet once they had effectively neutralised the Daleks, the Movellans vanished from space. Their fate is unknown, and their origins are equally obscure. But someone, or something, must have created them...

There are several possibilities. Since the Movellan androids were humanoid, it's likely that they were made in the image of their creators. There are, of course, countless humanoid races in the universe, and it's very possible that the Movellans rebelled and destroyed the people who had made them. They had a very specific purpose: the destruction of the Daleks. So were they designed by a race such as the Time Lords, invented as part of another clandestine project to wipe out the Daleks? Or could the Movellans even have been created by the Daleks themselves, as part of their duplicates programme? Extraordinary as it may sound, there is some evidence to support the latter idea. The Daleks worked constantly to refine and improve their duplicates, and the Movellans displayed a knowledge of Dalek technology and history compatible with the idea of them being a slave race gone rogue. They even exhibited some similarities with Robomen, from their need for orders to the control helmets that they wore when in their spaceships.

## RECREATING DAVROS

Michael Wisher was unavailable, so David Gooderson took his place in *Destiny of the Daleks*. He wore the original mask, which had to be split up the back and a new chin made to accommodate the new actor's broader head. The mask had been on public display for the previous four years and was not in good condition – it was accidentally thrown away at the end of one day's recording.

## I Obey!

Most Daleks have few conversational skills. Except among the highest levels of the Dalek hierarchy, their occasional debates tend to conclude with a simple command: 'Do not dispute!' Dalek drones, in fact, tend to limit themselves to a handful of phrases, generally covering

themes such as their obedience, their confidence in their forthcoming victories and what they're going to do to anyone who isn't a Dalek. Among the most frequently heard are:

Exterminate! ▶▶ I obey! ▶▶ My vision is impaired! I cannot see! ▶▶ Daleks conquer and destroy! ▶▶ You will obey! ▶▶ Seek! Locate! Exterminate! ▶▶ You will be exterminated! ▶▶ We are the masters of Earth! ▶▶ We will get our power! ▶▶ Obey without question!

## EXTERMINATE...?

The Daleks' most famous exclamation is, of course, 'Exterminate!' Much like Sherlock Holmes's 'Elementary, my dear Watson,' however, it's a catchphrase that gained currency in the media and among the public some time before it was heard regularly in the series. As Dalek voice actor Nicholas Briggs points out, 'The Daleks did occasionally say "Exterminate!" right from the beginning, but it wasn't a chant, it wasn't a war cry.' Indeed, the words 'extermination' and 'exterminated' appear just five times in the first seven-episode serial, and the cry 'Exterminate!' not at all. *The Dalek Invasion of Earth*'s Black Dalek orders 'Exterminate him!' three times in a scene in the sixth episode, and its use grew during *The Chase* and *The Daleks' Master Plan*, but it was used interchangeably with alternatives such as 'Annihilate', 'Kill' and 'Fire', and was just as likely to appear in commands like 'Prepare to be exterminated.'

The word did, though, make frequent appearances in newspaper stories about the Daleks. As Nicholas says, 'By the time the Daleks came back in *Day of the Daleks* in 1972, "Exterminate!" had come into the public consciousness. Those making the programme assumed it should be there, so there the Daleks were, chanting "Exterminate! Exterminate!" for the first time in the show's history.'

# Daleks Don't Like Stairs

'If you're supposed to be the superior race of the universe, why don't you try climbing up after us?'

'Ideal place to fight Daleks, you know... Good stout walls, an upper storey, stairs... Daleks don't like stairs.'

'Stay where you are! Do not move!' 'The stairs!' 'You are the Doctor! You are the enemy of the Daleks! You will be exterminated! Exterminate! Exterminate! Exterminate! Exterminate! Exterminate!'

'Great big alien death machine. Defeated by a flight of stairs!'

'El-ev-ate!'

# DALEKMANIA

## Doctor Who Weekly

*TV Comic's* final *Doctor Who* comic strip appeared on 11 May 1979. Exactly five months later, and just under three weeks after the conclusion of *Destiny of the Daleks*, Marvel Comics published the first edition of *Doctor Who Weekly*. The new magazine presented a selection of feature articles recounting the previous sixteen years of television stories and the most significant companions and enemies – beginning, of course, with the Daleks. There were also three comic strips: the main strip followed the Fourth Doctor on a series of epic adventures, while the second strip presented retellings of classic science fiction stories like *The War of the Worlds*. The third was a 'back-up' strip, showing what various monsters got up to when the Doctor wasn't around. The first of these was 'The Return of the Daleks', a four-parter in which Skaro's finest infiltrate the production of a movie recounting their defeat on the planet Anhuat eight centuries earlier.

Three months later, the Daleks were back, this time facing Abslom Daak, a convicted criminal sentenced to life as a Dalek Killer. It's a job with a short life expectancy, but Abslom Daak, Dalek Killer would return to slice up Daleks with his trusty chain-sword many times over the years. His second story, 'Star Tigers', came just a couple of months later, but only briefly featured the Daleks, perhaps because they were about to make their debut in the main strip.

'The Dogs of Doom' ran from April to June 1980. The Daleks are using vicious Werelox to attack and weaken the New Earth system. The Doctor himself becomes infected by the creatures and turns into a Werelok. Unusually for the Daleks at this time, they are planning to identify useful characteristics of various fearsome beasts and copy those traits into themselves to create a stronger Dalek army.

A few months later, Abslom Daak returned in 'Star Tigers, Part Two', destroying a Dalek spacecraft hidden inside a volcano on the planet Paradise. By this time, *Doctor Who Weekly* had gone monthly, Tom Baker's departure from the TV series had been announced, and the *Doctor Who* comic strip was on the verge of exploring new and fantastical realms. The Daleks were about to vanish from its pages for almost a decade.

## Terry Nation's Dalek Special

On 25 October 1979, Target – publisher of the ongoing range of *Doctor Who* novelisations – released a 96-page paperback compiled and edited by former script editor Terrance Dicks. *Terry Nation's Dalek Special* was 'a compendium of their past triumphs, their early beginnings, their series and their latest adventure'. It gave a glimpse of the inner workings of a Dalek, alongside a handful of puzzles and the opportunity to cut pieces out of the book and

assemble them into a small paper Dalek. 'This part is tricky,' caution the instructions if you reach step 5 (the Shoulders).

The book opened with a 32-page short story written by Terry Nation, entitled 'The Secret Invasion'. Four children, turned away from a cinema showing *The Exorcist* because they are too young, get trapped in a London Underground station, where they run into four Daleks. The Daleks fire on two of them – using minimum power – and take them prisoner. They let the other two escape, though, and the kids take with them a 'Dalek message plate' containing an ultimatum for the authorities. The plucky children join forces with the military to defeat the alien invaders, attending a Ministry of Defence briefing meeting along the way. In a nod to 1974's brace of general elections, the Prime Minister they meet there is not Edward Heath: '"Of course it's not," Emilie said impatiently. "It's Mr Wilson's turn this month." Emilie knew about politics.'

## 'On the Icy Edge of the Galaxy…'

In 1966, Century 21 Records released a 21-minute 'mini-album' adaptation of the final episode of *The Chase*, with narration by Dalek voice actor David Graham. Aside from that, *Doctor Who* fans and viewers had no access to episodes after they'd been broadcast, other than the Target novelisations. That would change in 1983 with the advent of home video, but first came the autumn 1979 release by BBC Records & Tapes of *Doctor Who – Genesis of the Daleks*. The album was a 60-minute abridgement of the TV story, with Tom Baker providing original linking narration.

The release was given low-key promotion, with occasional plugs after *Doctor Who*'s closing credits and brief mentions in *Radio Times*. Then, in 1980, an advert started to appear in *Doctor Who Weekly*, in which the Doctor lands the TARDIS outside a record shop on Gamma-Ursa 9. Popping in, he finds a copy of *Genesis of the Daleks* (in the Alien Menace section). Sadly, it looks unlikely that he'll be able to buy it, because the store is run by two Daleks called Zorg and Org, and they – typically – just want to exterminate him.

How the Doctor escapes from Zorg and Org has never been revealed.

'GENESIS OF THE DALEKS' A COMPLETE DR. WHO ADVENTURE!

# THEY PLAY TOO WELL

📺 **THE FIVE DOCTORS**
**by Terrance Dicks**
Starring Peter Davison,
Jon Pertwee, Patrick
Troughton, Richard
Hurndall, William
Hartnell and Tom
Baker as the Doctor
**First broadcast:**
25/11/1983

During the Dark Times, the earliest Time Lords misused their powers in numerous ways, not least with the Time Scoop – a means of gathering other life forms from any spatio-temporal location and depositing them in Gallifrey's Death Zone to fight. The Time Scoop was used indiscriminately, aside from the stipulation that both the Daleks and the Cybermen were too deadly to be included in the 'games'. Millennia later, however, the Time Scoop saw operation again, as part of Lord President Borusa's scheme to secure immortality, and a lone Dalek was captured and imprisoned in a special containment area in the Death Zone, as were the First Doctor and his granddaughter. The Doctor and Susan escaped, but the Dalek was tricked into destroying itself.

# THE RETURN

The Dalek-Movellan war continued for several decades after Davros's capture on Skaro, but ended abruptly when the Movellans engineered their virus. Casualties were heavy and Dalek forces so depleted that they were now forced to make use of duplicate humans and hired mercenaries. Once again, the Supreme Dalek decided that the Daleks needed their creator. A Dalek battle cruiser attacked an Earth prison ship and released Davros. Briefed on the situation, Davros promptly recognised that he would need to genetically re-engineer the Daleks if they were to survive. But he also realised that he needed to resolve other fundamental problems with his creations, beyond their susceptibility to the Movellan virus: he already knew that the Daleks' strictly logical programming had ultimately proved a weakness; he was also outraged that the Daleks followed the orders of a supreme commander other than himself. He needed to restore the primacy of the Daleks' organic heritage, and he immediately set about

📺 **RESURRECTION OF THE DALEKS**
by Eric Saward
Starring Peter Davison as the Doctor
**First broadcast:**
08/02/1984–15/02/1984

doing just that, using mind-controlling chemicals to recruit a small force of humans and Daleks.

The Supreme Dalek now considered Davros unreliable and ordered his death, but Davros had anticipated this and released a sample of the Movellan virus. As the two Dalek factions clashed, the virus did its work, destroying both. Davros fled the scene in an escape capsule, but was himself infected with the virus. The virus targeted the bonded polycarbide of their Dalekenium casings – and the Dalek casings were based on Davros's own chair.

The Daleks at this time also – finally – knew about the Time Lords. Throughout their previous encounters with him, the Daleks had always assumed the Doctor was simply a brilliant human, a madman with a time-travelling box. Though they had

### TRACKING DALEK TIMELINES
42nd century ▶▶ The Dalek-Movellan war ▶▶ 46th century
4500 ▶▶ The Daleks resurrect Davros ▶▶ 4500
4590 ▶▶ The Daleks liberate Davros ▶▶ 4590

slowly grasped that he was 'more than human', the Doctor's true origins had remained a secret from them. Now, however, the Daleks were fully aware that the Doctor was one of the race of Time Lords from the planet Gallifrey – and the Supreme Dalek saw the Time Lords, not the Movellans or the humans, as the ultimate enemy. A plan was formulated to trap the Doctor then despatch duplicates of him and his companions to Gallifrey to assassinate the High Council.

The Daleks – and Davros – were determined to revenge themselves on the Doctor and supplant the Time Lords as the universe's foremost temporal power. The Time Lords had unwittingly fired the first shot in an unimaginable conflict when they deployed the Doctor at the Daleks' creation; now the Daleks planned to fire the second...

## RECREATING DAVROS

Terry Molloy took over the role from 1984, appearing in three stories. A new mask was sculpted by Stan Mitchell, and appeared to show the degenerative effects of ninety years of cryogenic suspension. Nicknamed 'Ena Sharples' by the production team, the mask gave Davros a fleshier, more jowly appearance, and allowed a wider range of facial expressions, something fully exploited by Terry Molloy.

# Dalek Duplicates

> Success! Paramount Success! It is completely
> indistinguishable from the original!

After the failure of their invasion of Earth in 2167, the Daleks created a duplicate of the Doctor. Programmed to rigidly obey its orders to infiltrate and kill the Doctor's party, it was convincing enough to fool Barbara and to leave Ian and Vicki uncertain which was the real Doctor. It could, though, be disabled fairly easily by removing a control circuit from its chest.

After the catastrophic depletion of Dalek forces caused by the Movellan virus, the Daleks came increasingly to depend on humanoid duplicates as their shock troops, preferring to withdraw their own units as soon as they came under attack. They were so convincing that the duplicates themselves were unsure whether they were real.

The duplicate army was based on real people, and all were capable of displaying a convincing simulacrum of their original personalities. Their conditioning was unstable, however; the duplicate called Stien, for example, gradually recovered memoires of his true self and eventually rebelled against his masters, operating the prison ship's self-destruct.

The duplicate troops were under the control of Commander Lytton, a mercenary from Riften 5. Lytton himself was not a duplicate, but he had been conditioned, and the Supreme Dalek ordered his death when he overrode that conditioning.

The Supreme Dalek also placed duplicates in Earth's government in preparation for an invasion. The destruction of the Dalek battle cruiser meant that their activation signal was never sent, so the unstable duplicates' conditioning deteriorated and they reverted to their original personalities or were unmasked.

# THE END OF THE ROAD

📺 **REVELATION OF THE DALEKS**
**by Eric Saward**
Starring Colin Baker as the Doctor
**First broadcast:**
23/03/1985–30/03/1985

Davros found a way to re-engineer his systems and survive his infection by the Movellan virus. Establishing himself as the Great Healer on the planet Necros, he now set about building a new Dalek army. The organic component came from mutated humans – Necros was the location of Tranquil Repose, a funeral home for the wealthy and powerful, and Davros experimented on the dying to create new Dalek creatures. Unused flesh was converted into a high-protein concentrate with which he had all but eliminated famine – the Great Healer was widely regarded as a great benefactor by eager consumers who had no idea of the source of the foodstuff.

Some of his staff on Necros, however, did resist. Two of Tranquil Repose's orderlies summoned the Daleks from Skaro. Davros's Daleks were overpowered, and Davros was taken to Skaro for trial.

### TRACKING DALEK TIMELINES
4500 ≫≫ The Daleks resurrect Davros ≫≫ 4500
4590 ≫≫ The Daleks liberate Davros ≫≫ 4590
47th century ≫≫ Davros builds a new Dalek army on Necros ≫≫ 47th century

## Glass Dalek

A glass Dalek casing was part of the incubation process for the Daleks that Davros manufactured on Necros. The mutant head of Arthur Stengos was found by his daughter in this transparent casing – he was undergoing conditioning and reprogramming. This was the penultimate stage in the evolution of the Daleks on Necros, as a new Dalek shell appeared to grow up inside the glass Dalek, ready to house the finished mutant creature.

## The Search for Davros

> Once again, the Daleks have come back to me.. like an errant child.

After the Doctor's intervention in their creation, the Daleks became more dependent on Davros. They were never heard to mention him in their original timeline; it seems likely that the Daleks exterminated him then forgot all about him.

Perhaps it was the additional genetic modifications that Davros made in light of the Doctor's presence, or perhaps it was simply being entombed with his body after the Kaled bunker was sealed off – whatever the explanation, the Daleks of the new timeline did not forget their creator. The Supreme Dalek realised that the stalemate in the Movellan war had been caused by Davros's original programming of the Daleks, and concluded that the Movellan virus would be overcome only if the creator could somehow re-engineer the Daleks at their most fundamental level.

Davros rejected the upstart 'Supreme' and quickly came to his own conclusions about the need for a radical overhaul of his offspring. He appeared to bear them no ill-will for killing him, instead vowing not to allow himself the luxury of death until they were the supreme beings – with him at their head.

The squad of Daleks sent to retrieve him from Skaro all perished, and the entire battle cruiser that liberated him from the Earth prison ship was destroyed. Davros had proved himself unreliable through his attempts to build his own personal army of chemically controlled Daleks. Subsequently establishing himself on Necros, Davros was little more than an irritant, but he held the true prize – a growing force of desperately needed Dalek troops.

# NEMESIS

📺 **REMEMBRANCE OF THE DALEKS**
by Ben Aaronovitch
Starring Sylvester McCoy as the Doctor
**First broadcast:**
05/10/1988–26/10/1988

There were no non-Skaroene witnesses to the events that next unfolded on the Dalek home world, but Davros's trial did not go as the Supreme Dalek had expected. Before long, Skaro was controlled by the new breed of Imperial Daleks, under the command of their Emperor – Davros himself. Davros recast the other faction as Renegade Daleks, and these fled Skaro.

Both factions were at the height of their powers, technical and temporal. Each side moved mighty battle fleets at will through time corridors to different points in history, each manoeuvring to gain an advantage over the other and dominate all of time and space. The culmination of the conflict came in London on 1960s Earth.

Centuries earlier in his own timeline, the Doctor concealed a dangerous piece of Time Lord science in 1960s London. When he had absconded from Gallifrey, he took with him the Hand of Omega, a stellar-manipulation device that could turn a sun supernova. It was this device that had detonated the star from which Gallifrey now drew its power, but the Doctor recognised its potential as an ultimate weapon. Now he used it to spring a trap for the Daleks, and was a little disconcerted to discover that he'd ensnared two factions of them.

The Doctor's priority now was to prevent human casualties in the midst of the warring Daleks. Finally, the Imperial Daleks secured the Hand of Omega and left Earth. Addressing the Dalek mothership in orbit above the planet, the Doctor begged Davros not to use the stellar manipulator. Davros, convinced he now had the means to create a power source for unlimited time travel, triggered the Hand – which the Doctor had pre-programmed. It turned Skaro's sun supernova, obliterating Skaro in the process, before homing in on the Dalek mothership and destroying that. Davros managed to access an escape capsule moments before the explosion, but the Daleks were, to all intents and purposes, extinct.

## TRACKING DALEK TIMELINES

47th century ➤➤ Davros builds a new Dalek army on Necros ➤➤ 47th century ➤➤ The Daleks split into Imperial and Renegade factions ➤➤ 47th century ➤➤ Skaro destroyed by the Hand of Omega ➤➤ 47th century

# DALEK HIERARCHY
## The Supreme Daleks

By the start of the 46th century, the Daleks were ruled by a Supreme Dalek – whether or not the Daleks had avoided a Civil War in their current timeline, there was no longer a Dalek Emperor and no sign of a Supreme Council or the gold-coloured Commander rank. This Supreme Dalek was distinguished by its black casing, and it retained a tier of Black Dalek commanders to direct specific operations.

When the Supreme Dalek despatched a taskforce to Skaro to excavate the Kaled city and retrieve their creator, Davros was unimpressed: 'Supreme Dalek! That is a title I shall dispute most vigorously. I created the Daleks. It is I who shall control their destiny. I am the Supreme Commander.'

Although the Supreme Dalek turned once again to Davros for assistance with the Movellan virus, he quickly realised that the Daleks' creator could not be trusted and ordered his extermination. Instead the Supreme Dalek himself was destroyed when his battle cruiser was caught in the blast from the exploding prison ship.

While Davros was setting up on Necros, a new Supreme Dalek assumed command on Skaro, to which the Daleks had now returned. Learning of Davros's location, the Supreme Dalek despatched a taskforce to apprehend him. They returned with rather more than their creator – Davros's new white Daleks were also taken to Skaro for conditioning. This may have been a mistake.

Davros now fulfilled his pledge to contest the leadership of the Daleks. His Daleks triumphed, and the Supreme Dalek was forced to abandon Skaro again, fleeing with what was left of his own loyal Daleks, labelled

Renegades by Davros. When the Seventh Doctor landed in 1960s London to spring his Hand of Omega trap, Davros's Imperial forces were circling Earth in a huge mothership, while the Supreme Dalek was in hiding, forced to enlist the support of human white supremacists. Once the Hand of Omega had done its work, the Doctor confronted the Supreme Dalek:

'You have been defeated. Surrender! You have failed. Your forces are destroyed, your home planet a burnt cinder circling a dead sun. Even Davros, your creator, is dead! You have no superiors, no inferiors, no reinforcements, no hope, no rescue! You're trapped, a trillion miles and a thousand years from a disintegrated home. I have defeated you. You no longer serve any purpose.'

His words had their intended effect: the Supreme Dalek self-destructed, bringing an end to the original line of Kaled-descended Daleks.

## EXTERMINATION

In the 1960s, the extermination effect was achieved by opening the aperture on the studio camera, which turned the entire picture negative. This was sometimes aided by set-up shots of the Dalek gun firing, in which a stamen-like centrepiece would be seen to flick in and out of the gun rod. This visual effect remained the same until the introduction of colour television recording gave the negative shots a bluish tinge.

*Genesis of the Daleks* retained this negative effect, but brought in a special effect for the Dalek death ray – a tight blue beam of light. In *Destiny of the Daleks*, advances in video-editing technology meant that for the first time the negative effect played just around the victim. In *Remembrance of the Daleks*, a new visual effect was introduced: the full impact of a Dalek gun lit up the victim's body so that a negative image of its skeleton was revealed.

## Imperial Daleks

An entirely new race of Daleks was created by
Davros on Necros in his ultimately successful
bid to take control of the Dalek Empire. Their
distinctive casings were predominantly white,
with gold hemispheres. Programmed to be totally
obedient and loyal to Davros himself, they were
initially grown from the human bodies placed in
storage on Necros. When Davros was captured by the Supreme Dalek's
forces, these Daleks were taken back to Skaro for reconditioning to obey
the Supreme Dalek – a process which failed. Instead the new Daleks gained
control of Skaro with Davros as their Emperor, resulting in the exile of the
Supreme Dalek and his remaining forces.

## Special Weapons Dalek

The Special Weapons Dalek was a specially
modified Imperial Dalek that was fitted with
an enormously powerful gun and no other
attachments. It was essentially a Dalek tank,
suitable for all terrains and used on the front line of
any conflict. Unlike the Daleks themselves, Davros
was clearly prepared to adapt his Dalek design in
any way necessary to ensure their ultimate triumph.

## Dalek Factionalism

The Daleks project an image of a giant, uniform army, unquestioningly
obedient and united behind a single purpose. They operate under a strict
hierarchy, with orders issued by its upper echelons and obeyed without
question. Dissent has been programmed out of them, leaving them
genetically ill-equipped to deal with discussion and debate. They are
analytical creatures, with binary thought processes, resulting in an inability
to compromise, or even to acknowledge another point of view. The belief in
their ultimate superiority over all non-Dalek beings is hard-wired into their
positronic brains. Yet every individual Dalek is also able to reason and, for
much of their history, they have had the capacity to understand and exploit
the emotional fallibilities of other species.

So the Dalek race has an in-built weakness: they have the potential
to disagree, but the logical consequence of any dissent is a complete
breakdown of their society. The Daleks are a race perpetually on the brink
of civil war. In fact, almost their first act after their creation was to turn
on their maker and attempt to kill him. When the Human Factor spread
through the Daleks on Skaro, their programming for unthinking obedience
was undermined – the simple question 'Why?' became dangerous. The

Black Daleks lost their authority as the humanised Daleks rejected their orders, and the loyal Daleks responded in the only way they knew – by turning their guns on their fellow Daleks. Even the Emperor was ignored as he commanded them to stop fighting.

The reawakened Davros was quick to realise the limitations of his creatures' thought processes, and he immediately proposed creating a modified Dalek race, capable of more independent thought. Given the opportunity, in the laboratories of his prison ship, he made two test specimens, using chemicals to make them compliant with his instructions. The result was inevitable: the two Dalek factions destroyed each other.

When Davros was later apprehended with his new Dalek force on Necros, the resulting civil war was as much about thought crime as genetic re-engineering. Such were the losses to the Supreme Dalek's forces caused by the Movellan virus that it was decided to recondition Davros's Daleks, despite their inferior genetic origins. This fatal mistake left the Supreme Dalek's forces refugees in time, forced to try and counter the freer-thinking Daleks of Davros by using a human being to run their battle computer.

## DALEKMANIA

### The Ultimate Adventure

In 1989, Terrance Dicks was commissioned to write the third official *Doctor Who* stage play. He was given an ambitious list of things to fit in, including the Daleks, the Cybermen, a magic trick and three songs.

When the American Ambassador is

kidnapped from a nightclub, the British Prime Minister sends the Doctor, Jason, Krystal and Zog across time to rescue him. Along the way they battle flying aliens, a meteorite storm, and the duplicitous Madam Delilah. The Doctor realises that the Daleks and the Cybermen have formed an alliance with alien mercenaries, an alliance that begins to crack when Madam Delilah is exterminated in Bar Galactica. The Doctor is able to provoke the mercenaries and the Cybermen into rebellion, leading to the destruction of the Emperor Dalek. He returns to Earth and saves Margaret Thatcher from being blown up by the hypnotised Ambassador. Krystal abandons a promising singing career to continue travelling with the Doctor.

The show toured the country with first Jon Pertwee and then Colin Baker reprising their roles as the Third and Sixth Doctors. It featured some remarkable-looking Dalek props, which were apparently based on the build-your-own Dalek instructions published by *Radio Times*.

# THEY WENT OFF TO FIGHT A BIGGER WAR

T owards the end of his seventh life, the Doctor received a summons from the Master – the Doctor's rival was about to be executed by the Daleks, and his last request was that his remains be returned to Gallifrey. So the Doctor set the TARDIS controls for the planet Skaro.

📺 **DOCTOR WHO**
**by Matthew Jacobs**
Starring Paul McGann and Sylvester McCoy as the Doctor
**First broadcast:** 27/05/1996

That the Skaroene system was back in place in time for the Master's trial, late in the Seventh Doctor's timestream, suggests that Skaro was resurrected at some point after the detonation of its sun. The restoration of Skaro and the concomitant damage to the timelines may even have been

a decisive stage in the 'phony war' between the Daleks and the Time Lords that began when the Doctor was sent to prevent their genesis...

Some time after the Master's trial, the Emperor of the Daleks led his renewed race to become truly the greatest threat to the universe. The Daleks had grown in power and technological ability and now waged war on the cosmos, and especially on the human race, in a period of aggression that culminated in the Tenth Dalek Occupation.

After which... nothing. The Daleks vanished from time and space.

WIL REES DAVROS '74

### TRACKING DALEK TIMELINES

47th century ➤➤ Skaro destroyed by the Hand of Omega ➤➤ 47th century
c.5725.2 (Rassilon Era) ➤➤ Skaro restored ➤➤ c.5725.2 (Rassilon Era)
? ➤➤ The Tenth Dalek Occupation ➤➤ ?
? ➤➤ The Daleks vanish from time ➤➤ ?

Despite having engineered Skaro's destruction by the Hand of Omega, the Doctor seemed unsurprised by the planet's presence. It is possible that the Master's trial took place at a point in time before Skaro's demise – there are no records to confirm or deny this, and events were to follow that would not only dwarf the Doctor's many battles with the Daleks; the coming war would also shred the Daleks' already tangled timelines. Temporal powers, however, exist relative to one another within the causal nexus. The precise strictures of the Laws of Time are now lost, but seem to apply as much to the Daleks as they do to Time Lords like the Doctor and the Master.

WIL REES '96

In December 1989, *Doctor Who* began a sixteen-year absence from television, during which its legend was kept alive by home video and DVD releases of classic stories. At the same time, *Doctor Who Magazine* (as *Doctor Who Weekly* had eventually become), Virgin Publishing, BBC Books, Telos Publishing and Big Finish Productions were producing ever-growing licensed ranges of comic strips, novels, novellas and audio plays, extending the mythos and continuing the lives of all seven Doctors. From time to time, episodes from the archive would appear on BBC television, among them *Planet of the Daleks* and *Revelation of the Daleks*, plus a couple of showings of *Genesis of the Daleks*, often supported by documentaries and theme nights celebrating the long-running, long-loved and now long-lost series. The show's future now seemed to lie in expanding its past.

Then, for one night only in May 1996, a new Doctor took over BBC One. Paul McGann's Eighth Doctor didn't meet the Daleks, though they did feature – sort of – in the story's opening moments. But he might have done, had things gone differently...

The *Doctor Who* television movie had a difficult seven-year gestation that involved several arms of the BBC and various US television and film companies. By the time it entered production, several outlines, draft scripts and story ideas had been prepared and discarded. It was hoped that the movie would act as a pilot for a possible series, and the Daleks – and Davros – would, of course, have been foremost among the Doctor's adversaries. But these new Daleks would have been very different. The technology was now available to produce considerably more sophisticated imaginings of their potential, and the writers and producers were envisaging a highly mobile and flexible race of cyborg-mutants, their protective casings now a form of armour that could be adapted for different battles situations, including airborne combat. These 'Spider Daleks' would have had six-legged casings, from which their mutant controller could emerge, brandishing claws and talons and deadly weaponry. Davros meanwhile was imagined as an incredibly old humanoid sitting on a throne.

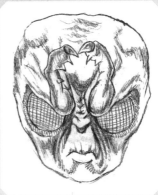

A number of conceptual drawings were prepared showing possible realisations of these ideas.

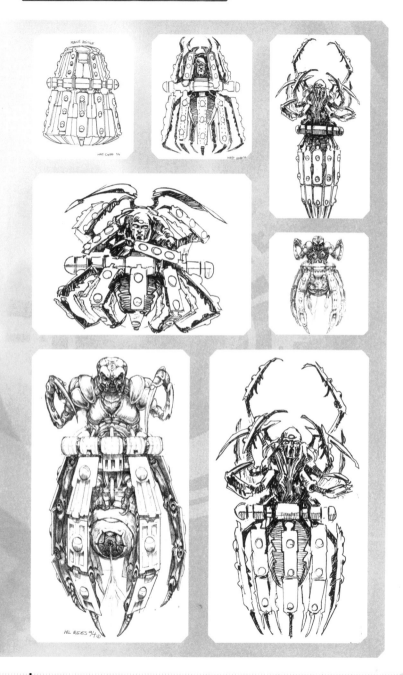

# DALEKMANIA: EXTENDING THE MYTH

## The Comic Strips

Nine years after their appearance in 'Star Tigers', the Daleks finally resurfaced in *Doctor Who Magazine*'s comic strip. In 'Nemesis of the Daleks', the Doctor joins forces with Abslom Daak, Dalek-Killer, who sacrifices himself to prevent the Daleks building a genocide machine capable of gassing entire planets.

'Bringer of Darkness' (1993) features the Second Doctor, who ruthlessly destroys an isolated Dalek patrol. Also published in 1993, 'Emperor of the Daleks' neatly explains what happened between *Revelation* and *Remembrance of the Daleks*. Davros promises to reintroduce emotions into the Daleks and make them a force for good, so the Sixth Doctor rescues him from his trial on Skaro. This prompts the Daleks to resurrect Abslom Daak and trick him into capturing the Seventh Doctor. The Daleks force him to reveal Davros's location – the planet Spiridon, where Davros has reconditioned the frozen Dalek army. A battle ensues between the two Dalek factions. Davros successfully conquers Skaro then reneges on his deal with the Doctor, who decides to mention a powerful device known as the Hand of Omega...

In 1996, a one-off special called 'Daleks v the Martians' brought back Dr Who as played by Peter Cushing in the 1960s movies. He, Susan and Louise travel to Mars in *Tardis*, where they help the natives use a Martian Sphinx – actually a deadly weapon – to repel a Dalek taskforce.

The following year, *DWM* resurrected and continued *The Daleks* – the strip that had run in *TVC21* more than thirty years earlier. Illustrated by one of the original artists, Ron Turner, 'Return of the Elders' picks up the story where the original strips left off – the Daleks enter Earth's solar system and begin their first

assaults on humanity. This was intended as an ongoing series, but Turner's death left the project unfinished.

May 1997 saw the Eighth Doctor's first encounter with the Daleks. 'Fire and Brimstone' begins with the Doctor obstructing a Dalek attack on a human satellite, but rapidly expands to reveal that the Daleks have a new enemy – the Threshold.

The Eighth Doctor had one further comic-strip encounter with the Daleks. This time, in 2002's 'Children of the Revolution', he is re-meeting old 'friends': the surviving humanised Daleks from *The Evil of the Daleks*. They have built a new, comparatively peaceful society, concealed in the oceans of the planet Kyrol. But these Daleks have been telepathically manipulated by Kata-Phobus, an aquatic, tentacled creature that feeds on the Daleks' psychokinetic energy and intends to use the Daleks to attack human colonies. The humanised Daleks sacrifice themselves rather than become the creature's weapon.

## The Computer Games

The first *Doctor Who* computer game was released by BBC Computers in 1983, and a handful of other attempts followed, all Dalek-free. Then, in 1992, came *Dalek Attack* from Alternative Software: 'The Earth Year 2254, the planet Skaro. Davros, in the presence of the Emperor Dalek, addresses his Battle Command: "Over the past 100 years we have witnessed the human race advance their scientific knowledge to the point of becoming a threat. It is time for the problem to be rectified." The Invasion Begins...'

The game featured Davros leading an invasion of the Earth. Various incarnations of the Doctor could be used to defeat his cunning plan, which made use of bombardment, Ogrons, Robomen, and almost every form of Dalek ever seen, including flying film Daleks and the

Special Weapons Dalek. If you won, the game ended with Davros 'frozen in time and space... for ever?'

In the wake of the Paul McGann TV movie, BBC Multimedia produced a new game in which players explored the TARDIS while trying to release the Doctor's incarnations from a psychic domain created by the Master. A particular highlight of *Destiny of the Doctors* was the sight of 3D Daleks patrolling the TARDIS corridors. It featured specially recorded voiceovers from several Doctors, and extensive new scenes with Anthony Ainley as the Master. The game was written by future script editor Gary Russell. 'It was tricky. Everything in the game bar the Doctor's dialogue and all the new Ainley material was sampled from TV episodes. We couldn't record

anything new, so half my life was spent trawling through old videos for samples and boring everyone senseless with my cries of "Listen to this, *this* is great *Doctor Who*..." It was scary. Would it work? Would anyone make it all the way through the database? Would the Daleks look good? And, for 1997, I think they did.'

Players defeated the Daleks by blowing them up with Dalekenium – something pioneered on TV in 1964 by London's rebels in *The Dalek Invasion of Earth*. If an attack worked, the Daleks would spin round and scream.

## The Novels

BBC Books began its monthly series of Eighth Doctor novels in June 1997, and among the first dozen releases were two books by writer John Peel, who had worked closely with Terry Nation on *The Official Doctor Who and the Daleks Book* published in the USA in 1988.

*War of the Daleks* has the Thals aiding Davros's escape from the Daleks in order to overthrow Dalek Prime, one of the last remaining original Daleks. The book aimed to tie up various issues of Dalek continuity, suggesting that the Skaro destroyed in *Remembrance of the Daleks* was actually a carefully created duplicate. Interviewed on publication, Peel revealed that he had originally devised the novel as a proposal for a four-part TV story. He was keen to complete the Davros-Dalek civil war thread that had run through the Daleks' last few television stories, while Terry Nation requested that he find a way to undo the destruction of the planet Skaro.

*Legacy of the Daleks* was a sequel to *The Dalek Invasion of Earth*. The Doctor is reunited with his granddaughter Susan. They fail to stop the Master activating a Dalek race bank buried in the old mine workings in Bedfordshire, and before long a new Dalek army is massing.

## The Curse of Fatal Death

Produced as part of the BBC's *Comic Relief* charity night in 1999, *The Curse of Fatal Death* was the first time computer-generated Daleks were seen on television. Broadcast in short episodes during the telethon, the big cliffhanger involved the Doctor throwing open a set of doors to reveal an enormous Dalek army.

The Master is working with the Daleks again in order to conquer the universe with a Zectronic Beam. Realising that Daleks have no sense of smell, the Doctor attempts to talk to his old foe via Tersuran flatulent linguistics. The Daleks are defeated, and the Doctor and his companion Emma are heading off to get married when they are stopped by a plea from the Daleks to prevent a Zectronic overload. 'What better way to end my career than by saving you metal gits?' announces the Doctor, losing his remaining lives in the process. The Daleks, devastated by the death of their greatest enemy, vow to reform. The Doctor regenerates into a woman and promptly falls in love with the Master.

*The Curse of the Fatal Death* was written by future *Doctor Who* showrunner Steven Moffat and starred Rowan Atkinson, Richard E. Grant, Jim Broadbent, Hugh Grant and Joanna Lumley as the Doctor, with Jonathan Pryce as the Master and Julia Sawalha as Emma.

## The Audio Plays

Since 1999, Big Finish Productions have been releasing the continuing adventures of Doctors Five to Eight, starring Peter Davison, Colin Baker, Sylvester McCoy and Paul McGann. The range of full-cast audio plays has been supplemented with a number of spin-off projects, allowing new stories featuring the first four Doctors to be added to the mix.

The Daleks have appeared regularly, attacking the Library of Kar-Charrat, Gallifrey, Zaleria (formerly Spiridon), a fictional Spiridon on the planetoid YT45, WBliss, the Amethyst Viral Containment Station, the Vault of Stellar Curios, Red Rocket Rising, the city of Lavonia and the Braxiatel Collection. The Doctors have also encountered them many times on Earth: during their 22nd-century invasion, and in a timeline in which it never happened; in a near future in which Shakespeare is disappearing from history; in an alternative timeline where the British Empire never fell; and in the village of Stockbridge. The Sixth Doctor has discovered what Davros was doing before taking over Necros, and subsequently prevented him from building an army of Mechonoids to wipe out the Daleks in the wake of *Revelation of the Daleks*. The Eighth Doctor also encounters Davros some time after *Remembrance of the Daleks*, finding that the Daleks' new Emperor has become insane. A *Doctor Who Unbound* takes the TARDIS to an alternative future for Skaro, in which Davros has betrayed the Daleks to the Quatch; while another *Unbound* reality contains a race known as Thaleks... Big Finish have also adapted three *Doctor Who* stage plays for audio, as well as producing a version of Terry Nation's script for the aborted 1967 US television series, *The Daleks*.

The Daleks appear in :

**DOCTOR WHO** ❱❱ The Genocide Machine ❱❱ The Apocalypse Element ❱❱ The Mutant Phase ❱❱ Seasons of Fear ❱❱ The Time of the Daleks ❱❱ Neverland ❱❱ Jubilee ❱❱ Davros ❱❱ The Juggernauts ❱❱ Terror Firma ❱❱ Return of the Daleks ❱❱ Renaissance of the Daleks ❱❱ The Davros Mission ❱❱ Brotherhood of the Daleks ❱❱ Enemy of the Daleks ❱❱ Patient Zero ❱❱ Plague of the Daleks ❱❱ The Four Doctors

**THE NEW EIGHTH DOCTOR ADVENTURES** ❱❱ Blood of the Daleks ❱❱ Lucie Miller ❱❱ To the Death

**THE COMPANION CHRONICLES** ❱❱ Fear of the Daleks

**THE STAGE PLAYS** ❱❱ The Seven Keys to Doomsday ❱❱ The Ultimate Adventure ❱❱ Curse of the Daleks

**DOCTOR WHO: THE LOST STORIES** ❱❱ The Daleks: The Destroyers

**DOCTOR WHO UNBOUND** ❱❱ Masters of War

**PROFESSOR BERNICE SUMMERFIELD** ❱❱ Death and the Daleks

## Dalek Empire

Beyond Big Finish's main *Doctor Who* range, there has also been a spin-off – a four-series Dalek epic written by Nicholas Briggs.

'The idea for *Dalek Empire* was to do something a little bit inspired by *TVC21* and the old Dalek annuals, where the Daleks were attacking the whole of human civilisation but the Doctor wasn't there to help,' explains Nicholas. 'It raised the stakes, making the Daleks more dangerous – without this Time Lord around who's always sure to defeat them. It was more like a classic Second World War drama, with a feeling that any of the main characters could be killed at any moment. In the first couple of series, it was a love story between two characters wrenched apart by the Dalek invasion. I thought, since the Daleks have only negative emotions, that it would be a strong thing to do to have their evil natures contrasted with the finest of human feelings.'

*Dalek Empire* features its own set of likeable, fallible, clever and treacherous

characters: Susan Mendes (Suz), the mysterious Kalendorf, and Alby Brook – a space pilot who falls in love with Suz just as the Daleks invade. But the real stars are the Daleks. 'The Daleks can never actually be the heroes. But they feature far more than they would in a *Doctor Who* story. I don't think the story ever makes you want them to win. In many ways, the Daleks in *Dalek Empire* are the nastiest they've ever been. The emphasis is on their cleverness and cunning plots. Also, there is always this feeling that they are a relentless force for evil that is bit-by-bit defeating the human race. The humans are in retreat and the Daleks are moving ever forward. They are a race that believes in its destiny of conquest. They've studied their enemies and worked out exactly how to manipulate and defeat them.

'I'm really proud of the conversations between Susan Mendes and the Dalek Supreme. And I particularly like the way Suz, effectively a holocaust survivor, has to choose whether or not to work for the Daleks in the short term and plan for victory later, or merely sacrifice herself in a pointless gesture of defiance. The way that Suz ends up being proud of her work for the welfare of Dalek slaves throws up all sorts of meaty, moral issues, which gives the stories a real, intriguing depth and makes the series very unpredictable. That's always a good thing. Keep the audience guessing. Keep changing the rules. Challenge people's expectations.'

One of the biggest surprises is the cliffhanger finale to the first series, with the Daleks breaking through into another universe and meeting Alternative Daleks, creatures so sickened by them that they immediately declare war. But the Alternative Daleks aren't a simple force for good. 'They're an alternative-universe version of the Daleks. They weren't created by a man, but a woman, called the

Mentor. They are similar to the Daleks of our universe, but they believe in establishing peace and cooperation. However, they're so convinced they're right, they are willing to take military action in order to enforce their ideals... The question is, at their core, are they really any less nasty than "our" Daleks?'

*Dalek Empire* swept on for four series, with David Tennant and Noel Clarke guest starring in the last two. It told a variety of stories – packing in an incredibly high body count, a grotesque return for the Varga plants, and a good deal of explosions and screaming. And, at the end of it, there's not quite a happy ending – the Daleks are never defeated. 'I don't know what happens in the end,' admits Nick. 'But I think they always come back. That's in the nature of evil.'

**DALEK EMPIRE** ➤➤ Invasion of the Daleks ➤➤ The Human Factor ➤➤ 'Death to the Daleks!' ➤➤ Project Infinity

**DALEK EMPIRE II** ➤➤ Dalek War Chapter One ➤➤ Dalek War Chapter Two ➤➤ Dalek War Chapter Three ➤➤ Dalek War Chapter Four

**DALEK EMPIRE III** ➤➤ The Exterminators ➤➤ The Healers ➤➤ The Survivors ➤➤ The Demons ➤➤ The Warriors ➤➤ The Future

**SHORT TRIPS: DALEK EMPIRE** (short stories)

**DALEK EMPIRE IV** ➤➤ The Fearless Part 1 ➤➤ The Fearless Part 2 ➤➤ The Fearless Part 3 ➤➤ The Fearless Part 4

## I, Davros

➤➤ Innocence ➤➤ Purity ➤➤ Corruption ➤➤ Guilt

In another Big Finish spin-off, the full story is told of Davros's life before *Genesis of the Daleks*. The series follows Davros from his teenage years, revealing details of his family – including his politically scheming mother, utterly devoted to her son's future pre-eminence. Davros himself is already demonstrating his academic and scientific brilliance, as well as his single-minded and emotionally detached approach to life and war on Skaro. By the end of *I, Davros*, the Kaleds' chief scientist has been crippled in an explosion and is engineering the birth of a new race and starting to devise life-support systems for them based on his own chair. Intriguingly, the first mutant creature to be installed in the Mark I travel machine is not a Kaled at all – but a Thal...

## The Novella

A series of *Doctor Who* novellas produced by Telos Publishing culminated in *The Dalek Factor*, written in 2004 by the award-winning horror author Simon

Clark. The Doctor is a prisoner of the Daleks, and has been for a very long time. Amnesiac and uncertain even of his own identity, he continues to frustrate the Daleks by helping their Thal prisoners to escape, unaware that the Daleks have outwitted him – each Thal has been implanted with the Dalek Factor and he is bringing them another step closer to winning at last...

# THE LAST GREAT TIME WAR

The details of the Time War are more obscure than anything else in the murkily entwined histories of the Daleks and the Time Lords. The War erupted through every time and no time and left the universe in an infinite state of temporal flux, yet no one knows how it started, few know what happened, and only one man truly knows how it ended.

Soon after the Tenth Dalek Occupation, the Daleks vanished from time and space. According to one account, the Dalek Emperor led his entire race into the Time Vortex and let loose the Deathsmiths of Goth, while the Time Lords were deploying a fleet of Bowships, Black Hole Carriers and N-Forms gathered from their own history. In the first year of the War, the Doctor witnessed Davros's death as his command ship flew into the jaws of the Nightmare Child at the Gates of Elysium.

As the universe convulsed, the Time War raged on. The Sontarans looked on enviously, excluded from what they regarded as the finest war in history, but other Lesser Species were entirely unaware of the way that the histories of their worlds were being changed and unchanged. Higher Species like the Forest of Cheem watched and despaired, and some were directly affected. The Nestenes lost not only their foodstocks, but also their protein planets. The bodies of the Gelth wasted away; they were reduced to a gaseous half-life, perpetually in search of a new corporeal form. One legend has it that the Greater Animus and its Carsenome were destroyed, and the Eternals left this reality entirely. The Doctor led the Time Lords in battle and fought on the front line. He witnessed the devastating fate of

Arcadia, and tried to save the Nestene home world and many others. He failed.

The unprecedented savagery of the War caused both Daleks and Time Lords to adapt rapidly. Now able to absorb the background radiation generated by time travel the Daleks began to use it as a power supply. The Time Lords resurrected one of their greatest criminals, the Master, to fight on their behalf – he was the perfect warrior in a Time War. But when he watched the Dalek Emperor take control of the Cruciform, the Master fled to the Silver Devastation, 100 trillion years in the future, and disguised himself as a human child, hoping never to be found.

On each side, principle was compromised. The Time Lords' policy of non-intervention now mutated into a complete disregard for the effects of their actions on weaker races. Entire planets, whole civilisations could be sacrificed in an instant, to save Gallifrey. By the end of the conflict, even the central Dalek ideals of genetic purity and uniformity had been weakened, and the Emperor had created a secret and autonomous order of Daleks. After the fall of Arcadia, this secret order escaped into the Void

with a stolen Time Lord prison ship containing millions of Daleks, awaiting an opportunity to return.

In the final days of the War, millions of lesser races died with every second that passed, only for Time itself to resurrect them, just to find new ways of dying, again and again. Unimaginable horrors, new and ancient, were born and reborn in the conflict: the Skaro Degradations, the Horde of Travesties, the Couldhavebeen King, the Army of Meanwhiles and Neverweres… The Time War had turned into Hell.

Gallifrey itself remained at the furthest edge of the Time War, but the final Dalek assault transformed the Time Lord home world. The mountains of Solace and Solitude burned, the valley between them a pit of fire, and the shattered hulls of downed Dalek spaceships littered the flaming landscape around the Time Lords' Citadel. The glass dome surrounding the Citadel was cracked, left open to the elements and, in the ancient edifices beneath, broken roofs and ancient stone and metal were aflame. The first Time Lord President, Rassilon, had been restored to life by a race now desperate for victory. He and his High Council retreated to a protected void, linked to the Citadel.

The Time Lords' determination to survive and their increasing megalomania had propelled them towards a devastating Final Sanction – a plan to rupture the Time Vortex and destroy all life in the universe, while they would ascend to become creatures of consciousness alone. The Time Lords would become non-corporeal beings, unaffected by time or cause and effect, and the rest of creation would be destroyed.

**THE END OF TIME**
by Russell T Davies
Starring David Tennant
as the Doctor
**First broadcast:**
25/12/2009–01/01/2010

With the entire war timelocked, so neither side could escape and no other beings could enter it, the Doctor took possession of something immeasurably powerful called simply 'the Moment' and disappeared. He now had the opportunity and means to end the Time War completely, and he chose to take it. Both great battle fleets, tens of millions of ships, and both home worlds were obliterated, and the Daleks and the Time Lords died burning and screaming in an inferno that lasted just a single second. The Doctor saw Gallifrey and Skaro reduced to rocks and dust, and walked away from the ruins entirely alone – the only survivor, as far as he knew, of the Last Great Time War.

# I CAN... FEEL

📺 **DALEK**
**by Robert Shearman**
Starring
Christopher Eccleston
as the Doctor
**First broadcast:**
30/04/2005

The Doctor's belief that he was the only survivor of the Time War proved unfounded. A Dalek ship – the damaged command ship of the Emperor – fell through time and hid in the dark space. For centuries, the Daleks rebuilt and plotted, hatching a twin scheme to repopulate the Dalek race while manipulating the human race into the loss of an empire Earth would never know it was supposed to have.

But the Emperor's saucer was not the only Dalek force to escape the War's final destruction. A lone Dalek also fell back through time, plummeting to Earth on Ascension Island in the second half of the 20th century. It burnt in its own impact crater for three days, screaming in pain.

Eventually, it was retrieved by human military forces, but soon passed into the hands of Earth's small circle of private collectors of alien ephemera. For the next few decades, it was sold at discreet auctions from one collector to another, none knowing what exactly they were buying, until it was bought by Henry Van Statten, billionaire boss of Geocomtex, owner of the internet and of one of the largest collections of extraterrestrial artefacts on Earth in the early 21st century. In all that time, the 'Metaltron', as Van Statten named it, remained silent and inert, only the faintest of life signs confirming that there was something inside the burnt and battered metal casing. Even sustained bouts of torture failed to provoke any reaction from the dormant creature.

**TRACKING DALEK TIMELINES**
**》》 THE TIME WAR 》》**
c.1960 》》 'The last Dalek' crashes on Ascension Island 》》 c.1960
2012 》》 'The last Dalek' breaks out of Van Statten's museum 》》 2012

The arrival in Van Statten's Utah base of the Doctor, however, revived the Dalek. It manipulated the Doctor's friend Rose Tyler into touching it – as a time traveller, Rose was soaked in the background radiation that the Dalek needed to restore itself to full power and functionality. It broke free from its cell and rampaged through the Geocomtex complex, killing hundreds of people and absorbing the whole power supply of North America's West Coast as well as all the human knowledge contained on the internet.

But that was not all the Dalek had absorbed – its genetic extrapolation from Rose had included not just background radiation but also human DNA. The Dalek quickly began to mutate, effectively becoming a new hybrid of Dalek mutant and human and inheriting some of Rose's compassion and pity – it was infected with the Human Factor. It had spent more than fifty years signalling for other Daleks, hoping for orders. Realising it was alone, and nurturing a confused hatred for its new self, the last Dalek self-destructed.

## BRINGING BACK THE DALEKS
### by Robert Shearman

Putting the Daleks before an entirely **new** audience of viewers, many of whom wouldn't even have been born the last time Daleks had squared off against the Doctor, meant that we couldn't just **tell** everyone they were important, and leave it at that. The difficulty with putting the Doctor up against an entire army is that you don't get to see them as individual characters. But introducing a single Dalek, all alone – and showing how complex it was, and how much personality it might have, and how **dangerous** it could be – would mean that you carry that impression in your head later. I wanted to take an ordinary, bog-standard, grunt Dalek – the sort of Dalek you'd normally see in background shots – and show everyone just how deadly one of those could be.

Traditionally, all we hear of a Dalek is when it's ranting. Exterminate! Seek, locate, destroy! It isn't given very much to introspection. It doesn't have time for it. (And thinking too much gets in the way of the ranting, so a Dalek wouldn't feel very comfortable doing it for too long – it'd seem disloyal to his military training!) But my Dalek has had a long time on his own, and a long time to be lost in his thoughts. So to have him actually *converse* with Rose – just for once, to have him speak with intonation, not just in a self-confident monotone – was thrilling for me. I wanted to show that even without the gun, even unable to move, the Dalek was still very, very dangerous. You don't want to talk to a Dalek. You don't want its cunning lies inside your head.

The most exciting moments were when I got to challenge all those lazy ways the Daleks had been mocked over the years. It was getting to use the sink plunger! It was getting them flying up stairs! And, most of all, it was that bit when the Dalek breaks its chains, and can stop play-acting, when it can exult in its own power once more. 'The Daleks survive in me!' I actually put off writing 'Exterminate!' – it was such a catchphrase, and I was so used to it, that I almost felt as if I were just back to being a kid and playing *Doctor Who* in the playground! I didn't feel worthy of it.

A lot of the real writing process was about not wasting the Doctor-Dalek confrontations. There are only three scenes where they get to talk in the entire story: at the beginning, in the middle, and at the end. And that is the story, really – getting to see how differently they behave to each other whenever they talk. So that first time the Doctor is frightened and appalled to find a Dalek has survived – and out of that fear comes this awful appalling desire for quick revenge. The second time, they're almost equals: I like to believe the Dalek has electrocuted all those soldiers in a couple of laser bolts just to show off, just to impress the Doctor (he's turned on the cameras deliberately so the Doctor can see). And as destructive as the Dalek is, it reaches out to the Doctor: his enemy is the one creature in the universe who might understand him, and is worthy  of talking to him, or of giving him orders. There's something so desperately pathetic in that need to impress, it makes the Dalek like a little kid. By the end, the Dalek has evolved still further – it has made moral decisions to spare the lives of those that tortured it, it has tried to deal with a new rush of feelings that are alien to it, and redefine what it is. By the time the Doctor points a gun at it, we ought to feel the Doctor's missed the boat a bit; that by being absent, he's not been filled in on that character progression. The Dalek is changing, and is suffering as a result of that change. It would rather die than be like us. Its only purpose is to hate and to kill us.

## ABSENCE OF THE DALEKS

In 2005 the Daleks hadn't been seen on screen for nearly twenty years. One of the first questions that the makers of the new series faced was 'Will the Daleks be in it?'

It was a good question. Behind the scenes, a formidable amount of discussion between the BBC and Terry Nation's estate was taking place to ensure that the Daleks made their triumphant return. For a while, negotiations over the minutiae of marketing, merchandising and international sales became so convoluted that it looked as though it wouldn't be completed in time for filming of the first series. But TV production schedules demand scripts, and writer Robert Shearman's task became even harder when the news was broken to him that he'd have to do a draft of *Dalek* that didn't contain a Dalek. Tricky, as Robert explains...

'My story is all about introducing an icon: it's all about declaring that the Dalek is big and is important and is familiar. Most of the dramatic moments in the episode come precisely out of those statements. It's not the way you'd characterise a new monster from scratch, it wouldn't make any sense. So the new script couldn't afford to trade off *Doctor Who* lore, it had to build up the danger around the monster better.

'Russell T Davies came up with this idea of a killer sphere, and that it would transpire in some later story that the spheres were the far-distant future evolution of the human race. He had the idea in reserve for some future series. He's very clever, Russell; I never knew how far he had *Doctor Who* mapped out in advance, but I suspect he had at least vague notions for right up until the end of David Tennant's Doctor! These spheres (as yet unnamed) would have been the opponents in the Time War, and the Doctor would never have known what they were. This would have provided a greater mystery for him to solve later in the series, and a greater emotional angst too – why did  these strangers destroy his race? Russell suggested I make my sphere mute, but I found it far too hard to sustain an entire story without it talking. I made its relationship with Rose very different; this sphere was a giggling child psychopath who delighted in sadism for its own sake. I think the script was a lot funnier, but far less moving. I prefer the one we ended up with!'

```
INT. SPHERE CELL

The DOCTOR bangs on the locked door.

                    DOCTOR
        Let me out!

The SPHERE recovers its speech quickly - somewhat rasping,
high-pitched like a child.

                    SPHERE
        It is the Doctor, isn't it?

The DOCTOR whirls round to face it.

                    SPHERE (CONT'D)
        The last of the Time Lords. The one that ran away.

                    DOCTOR
        (savagely) All right then. Finish the job.

                    SPHERE
        Before we've had a chance to chat?

                    DOCTOR
        If you can kill me, just kill me.

And the SPHERE pulls against its chains. With terrifying speed,
it swings out of its pit as far as it can, in front of the
DOCTOR's face.

                    SPHERE
        Do I frighten you, Doctor?

                    DOCTOR
        (softly) No.

                    SPHERE
        No need for lies, two friends like us. I can hear
        your hearts racing, pat-a-pat, pat-a-pat.

                    DOCTOR
        We wiped you out. You should be dead...

                    SPHERE
        Yes. Not though. Sorry.

                    DOCTOR
        What are you? (Beat.) You can't kill me. You can't
        do anything. Tell me what you are.

                    SPHERE
        It's so important to you?

                    DOCTOR
        I need to know.

                    SPHERE
        (sing-song) Don't think you're going to
        like it!
```

**'ABSENCE OF THE DALEKS'**
by Robert Shearman

**DOCTOR**

They rolled back through time, from a billion years in the future. And attacked. Every sentient species they could find, genocide on a universal scale. Nestenes, Daleks, their civilisations decimated, countless others completely wiped out.

**GUNTHER**

Why?

**DOCTOR**

I don't know. Don't you see, we never knew. My people trapped them on our planet, they had to be stopped somehow. Mutually assured destruction, we sacrificed ourselves to take them out. But it didn't work, did it? There's still one down there, it isn't over yet...!

**'ABSENCE OF THE DALEKS'**
by Robert Shearman

BYWATER fires, close blank range. And fires. And fires. The bullets hitting the SPHERE full on. It waits patiently until BYWATER has run out of ammunition, the gun clicking. He lowers the gun, now useless. He looks sick with fear.

**SPHERE**
Now. Let's have fun.

And immediately, with a clean sound of sharp metal, two blades extend from the base of the ball.

**'ABSENCE OF THE DALEKS'**
by Robert Shearman

When the Daleks returned in 2005, their bold new look was a team effort from Matt Savage at the *Doctor Who* Art Department and Mike Tucker, the Model Unit Director. Matt drew up concept art for every possible aspect of the new design, while Mike's unit was in charge of the actual construction of the full-size fibreglass prop.

'The original Dalek design was fairly extraordinary,' says Mike. 'They managed to nail pretty much the perfect monster on the first story – their first crack at an alien monster and they got to do the Daleks! All the decisions made at the time turned it into a 1960s design classic.'

When they began work in 2004, Mike was steered very firmly by showrunner Russell T Davies: 'Russell said, "In silhouette, you would just go *that's* a Dalek." The fact that we changed all the little details – no wire mesh around the shoulder, it's got rivets and facets on it that weren't there before – that's almost insignificant so long as the silhouette is there.'

Matt received similar guidance: 'Russell always said, "We are going to be doing a Dalek and you have to keep all the elements because otherwise you're going to be doing something else." In terms of structure and proportions, it was always going to be the same. The most difficult thing was going to be making them credible for a new audience, and looking at the textures – making them look like a metal tank rather than like something that was made in the prop shop.'

Once the design was signed off, the build was handed over by Matt to

Mike's team. 'No one knows a Dalek better than Mike Tucker,' says Matt. 'He sourced some of the original elements – the base and the spheres – and we sent him sketches, then he made a model and sent it back. It was a real two-way collaboration.'

From the start, Russell was keen for the new Daleks to look as if they were made from copper and bronze. 'They had to look solid. They had to look really heavy,' Mike recalls. 'I was slightly baffled as to why we weren't going for the silvers and blue-greys that had been used in the classic series. One of Matt's design drawings showed a gun-metal grey version of the new Dalek, and I thought it looked fantastic. Then, when I realised there'd be copper and bronze Daleks versus steel and grey Cybermen the next year, I understood perfectly.'

'We managed to make the casings look like they were metal,' confirms Matt. 'There were lots of surfaces on the original design that didn't have much going on, so we added things you'd find on machinery, like shut lines and rivets.' He does have one regret: 'The plunger stayed! I was very keen to do a claw for that, I'd really liked the claw on the movie Daleks, and we got that on a Dalek for *The Parting of the Ways*. I started doing designs for Daleks with claws, but when the script for *Dalek* came through, we realised it had to be a plunger – it's a piece of Dalek heritage, whether you like it or not!'

The enhancements to the original were influenced by the production team's love of all things Dalek, and Mike took a pick-and-mix approach to Dalek design. 'One of the first things that Russell said to us was "You need to make this look the most Daleky Dalek that's ever been seen – find all the bits that you like, whether they be from the films, the TV series, the comic

strips, the books... Whatever you find that you think has worked, put them on the new Dalek!" So, it's a real mish-mash of everyone's favourite bits of the Dalek.'

One example was Matt's love

of the Dalek comics. 'I was quite a big fan of the Dalek comics from the 1960s. Generally, they'd have a piece of graphic on them somewhere, and that felt like their serial code, so one of the things we thought we'd do was put Dalek graphics under the eyestalk so that when they looked at each other they could see who they were talking to.'

When first seen in *Dalek*, the prop was given a deliberately damaged and time-worn appearance, an effect which Mike feels enhanced the mechanical feel of it. 'With the really battered Dalek, we realised that if it was made of copper and bronze then we could go about adding greens and verdigris and really making it look as though it had oxidised and distressed over the years, and all that colour information and colour chaos on the prop really helped make it look like something that was made out of metal and not fibreglass.'

Matt was delighted with the finished result. 'The first time I saw the Dalek I'd worked on, I genuinely felt like I was 10 years old again. We went down to the Millennium Stadium where Mike Tucker had it all set up with the lights on and the operator inside. We went round a corner, and there it was – my first reaction was to run. After fear, my next response was pride. I was just immensely proud to have worked on something that was part of my childhood.'

'It will probably always be my calling card,' admits Matt, grateful to have had the chance to update Raymond Cusick's designs. 'In terms of the original design, we didn't alter anything. We were standing on the shoulders of giants.'

## VOICING AN ICON

'My main Dalek voice, the starting point, is heavily influenced by Peter Hawkins. He was brilliant. I also throw in a bit of Roy Skelton for good measure. Those guys were fabulous.'

When *Dalek* began recording in October 2004, Nicholas Briggs was chosen to give voice to the 'Metaltron'. He was present at the script read-through and throughout filming, his lines being heard by the actors on set, complete with ring-modulated electronic distortion. 'I watch the action on a monitor and then I just scream like mad, basically. The first time the cast heard me speaking as a Dalek was at the read-through. The first thing I had to do was a gut-wrenching scream. Christopher Eccleston tried to carry on, and then he stopped. He'd had no idea I was going to have a ring modulator there and he just pointed at it. A few lines later, I had my very first "Exterminate", and Chris went, "*Yes!*" and everyone else gave me a huge cheer.'

'The single prisoner in *Dalek* had a lot of very soft, plaintive material, and the trick was to push the envelope and make the Dalek genuinely pathetic, but also never lose sight of the fact that it was a Dalek. Russell T Davies and director Joe Ahearne were, I think, worried that it would just be ludicrous if it was too staccato. Russell phoned me the night before the big scene with Chris to tell me not to worry about sounding like a classic Dalek. Joe Ahearne kept asking me to do it quieter and slower. That pushing from both of them really helped, and I think we came up with something rather special.'

## The Last Dalek

*Doctor Who*'s renewed presence on BBC One since 2005 has been supplemented by an ever-growing range of supporting material – BBC Three's behind-the-scenes series *Doctor Who Confidential*, interactive mini-episodes on BBCi, brief episode preludes downloadable to mobile phones, and episode commentaries available on BBC Radio 7, on BBCi, and as podcasts from the official *Doctor Who* website. Long one of the most popular sections of bbc.co.uk, the website features backstage videos, photo galleries and selections of concept art, sound effects and games.

The first game devised for the 2005 series was *The Last Dalek*, made for the BBC site by the firm New Media Collective. Based on the scenario for *Dalek*, it saw players controlling the last Dalek as it tried to defeat the Doctor and escape from Van Statten's base.

With the show yet to air, secrecy was especially intense, so a courier had to travel down to the games company in Leeds with a copy of the episode (labelled *Ready Steady Cook* in case it fell into the wrong hands),

staying with the tape at all times while the New Media team took screenshots and made set measurements. The *Doctor Who* Art Department also supplied specially shot reference materials of the set. Dalek voices were recorded for the game by Nicholas Briggs.

Played by a million people in the month that it launched, the game was shortlisted for a 2005 British Interactive Media Association award.

# PURE AND BLESSED DALEKS

**THE LONG GAME**
**by Russell T Davies**
Starring Christopher
Eccleston as
the Doctor
**First broadcast:**
07/05/2005

Meanwhile, in another sector of time, the Emperor of the Daleks began to repair and rebuild his race. Concealed in dark space, he infiltrated Earth's Satellite Five. This orbiting space station retrieved, collated, edited and disseminated news from throughout the Fourth Great and Bountiful Human Empire. The Daleks had the Jagrafess secretly installed as puppet controller of Satellite Five and hence of Earth's news broadcasts. These were edited and manipulated to weaken and divide the Empire, redirecting its technological development and preventing its expansion.

In the year 200,000, the Doctor brought about an end to the Jagrafess's control of Satellite Five, but did not fully appreciate the effects of his actions. The news channels stopped broadcasting, and nothing replaced them – with no flow of information, Earth's government and economy broke down. Over the next century, environmental and economic collapse left half the population starving. Satellite Five was now known as the Game Station, and its game shows were compulsory viewing. Participants were randomly selected, and losing contestants were apparently disintegrated; they were in fact teleported to the Dalek command ship, where their flesh and organs were sifted for material to breed a new race of half-human Daleks. The new Daleks worshipped the Emperor, who came to regard himself as God. Despite this, the fundamental principle of genetic purity remained so strong in the Daleks, that they were driven insane by their own flesh.

The Doctor's arrival on the Game Station forced the Emperor to bring forward his plans, and he unveiled his new Dalek force: two hundred fully equipped spaceships, with two thousand Daleks aboard each one – almost half a million Daleks ready to destroy planet Earth. As the Daleks began to wipe out whole continents, the Doctor worked quickly to create a Delta Wave, knowing that it would annihilate not just the Daleks but all Earth's inhabitants too. In the end, the Doctor could not bring himself to operate the device so soon after killing his own kind. Earth was at the Daleks' mercy and the Doctor faced his final end.

📺 **BAD WOLF /
THE PARTING
OF THE WAYS**
**by Russell T Davies**
Starring Christopher
Eccleston as the Doctor
**First broadcast:**
11/06/2005–18/06/2005

But Rose Tyler, determined to save the Doctor, looked into the heart of the TARDIS and absorbed the energy of the Time Vortex. The unimaginable power transformed her into a godlike being, giving her the ability to shred every atom of the Emperor and his fleet. Every Dalek was obliterated in a matter of moments.

## The Game Station Controller

After the death of the Jagrafess, the Daleks replaced their puppet with a human they could regulate directly. The Controller was a living human computer interface, plugged into the satellite's systems at the age of 5. She monitored and directed all aspects of the Game Station and the

various game shows that it produced. She was blind and unable to move, processing a constant stream of data fed directly into her mind as a series of numbers. Her discovery that the Daleks feared the Doctor gave her hope that they could be defeated. She betrayed her masters, bringing the Doctor aboard the Game Station and giving him the spatial location of the Dalek fleet. She was transmatted onto the Dalek Emperor's command ship and exterminated.

## Playing the Long Game

> We waited here in the dark space, damaged but
> rebuilding. Centuries passed, and we quietly
> infiltrated the systems of Earth.

Many now extinct races have made the mistake of assuming the Daleks are straightforward warriors.

When the Doctor first visited Skaro, the Daleks' initial instinct was to allow the captured travellers to die of radiation sickness, but they reconsidered and allowed them to take anti-radiation medication. Susan was then tricked into luring the Thals into the Dalek city with an offer of food, water and an alliance. Once there, the Thal leader was exterminated.

The Daleks are always working towards a single objective – supremacy, and they are prepared to wait to achieve it. A full decade followed the bacteria bombardments that began the 2157 invasion of Earth before the Daleks were ready to complete Project De-Gravitate. The lone Dalek in Utah remained motionless and silent for fifty years awaiting an answer to its distress signal. After the Time War, the Emperor hid for centuries, his new Daleks driven mad by the silence then madder still by their human-tainted flesh. The Jagrafess ran Satellite Five for 91 years, slowly weakening Earth's empire as the Emperor Dalek regrew his forces. When that plan failed, the Emperor took advantage of the disarray on Earth, using the renamed satellite to continue the emasculation of humanity while increasing Dalek numbers as another century passed.

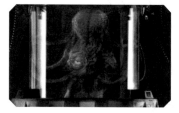

Equally, the Daleks are capable of swiftly changing a long-term plan: the Doctor's presence on the Game Station prompted the Emperor to advance their stratagem to invade Earth. Daleks exhibit extreme impatience as a project nears completion and are always intolerant of slow performance by slave workers – any last-minute delays will result in death.

Daleks can execute several complicated schemes simultaneously – their rescue of Davros from a prison ship so that he could work on an antidote to the Movellan virus ran alongside a scheme to capture and duplicate the Doctor in order to assassinate the High Council of Time Lords. This complexity of thought is part of their heritage from Davros, who established a business empire on Necros, cloned himself as a decoy for assassination attempts, and revelled in devising a complex trap for the Doctor.

Like their creator, Daleks may move in straight lines, but they rarely think in them.

# SURVIVING THE TIME WAR

aving detected a radar black spot in London, the Torchwood Institute discovered a spatial disturbance and initiated the design and construction of Britain's tallest building around it: Torchwood Tower, known to the public as the Canary Wharf tower at One Canada Square. The disturbance was a breach in the surface

**ARMY OF GHOSTS/ DOOMSDAY**
**by Russell T Davies**
Starring David Tennant as the Doctor
**First broadcast:**
01/07/2006–
08/07/2006

of the universe that led into the Void between parallel dimensions. When a Void Ship punched its way into this reality, Torchwood secured it in a specially constructed Sphere Room in the tower, unaware that it contained the Cult of Skaro and the Genesis Ark. The Time Lord prison

# DALEKMANIA

## I Am a Dalek

The Quick Reads range was developed to provide exciting, dramatic and funny stories, ideal for adults who've stopped reading or find reading tough, and for regular readers who want a short, fast read. The first books were published in May 2006 and included a *Doctor Who* novel featuring the Tenth Doctor and Rose Tyler: *I Am a Dalek* by Gareth Roberts, writer of a number of TV episodes.

Set after *The Parting of the Ways* and

before *Army of Ghosts*, it tells the story of Kate, whose latent Dalek heritage is reawakened when she's run over on the way to work. She reactivates a long-dead Dalek, a victim of the Time War, found on an archaeological dig and, as the Dalek itself grows in strength, she finds the Dalek Factor growing inside her. The Dalek's aim is to make Kate part of a servant race, containing enough Dalek DNA to help regrow a genuine Dalek species.

ship was inert and needed the touch of a time traveller to activate it. It seems likely that the Cult identified 21st-century London as a likely temporal and physical location at which to encounter the Doctor. They were right – the Ark was activated by an accidental touch from Mickey Smith, Rose's one-time boyfriend, and millions of Daleks streamed out to attack London.

What the Cult of Skaro had not expected was that another race would also exit the Void to invade Earth. Five million Cybermen from a parallel Earth had followed the Void Ship and systematically conquered the planet before the Cult of Skaro emerged. Even this number of Cybermen was insufficient to stop the Daleks, but the ensuing Battle of Canary Wharf did delay both aggressors just long enough for the Doctor to reopen the breach into the Void. Anything and everything that had existed within the Void was sucked back through the breach – every Cyberman and every Dalek. Almost every Dalek…

### TRACKING DALEK TIMELINES

200,000 ➤➤ The Daleks control the
Game Station ➤➤ 200,100
200,100 ➤➤ Dalek Emperor destroyed
by the Bad Wolf ➤➤ 200,100
2007 ➤➤ The Battle of Canary Wharf ➤➤ 2007

# TARDISODE

Throughout the 2006 series, each story was previewed in specially made one-minute preludes viewable online or via mobile phones. The *Tardisode* for *Doomsday* was released on 1 July, after *Army of Ghosts*:

**NEWSREADER**
This is an emergency broadcast. The country is under attack. The government has declared a state of emergency. We are awaiting more instructions. What do you mean, we've lost contact? What can I..? We have heard nothing more from the government. The Cybermen are everywhere. I don't know if anyone's watching this, but if you see them, run. Just run.
Mum – Dad – please. Please go..
This is Doomsday.

**DALEK**
We are the masters of Earth. Daleks conquer and destroy. Exterminate!

**TARDISODE: DOOMSDAY**
by Gareth Roberts

## The Cult of Skaro

**THE DOCTOR**
The last four Daleks in existence. So what's so special about you?

**ROSE**
Doctor, they've got names. And Daleks don't have names, do they? One of them said they—

**DALEK THAY**
I am Dalek Thay.

**DALEK SEC**
Dalek Sec.

**DALEK JAST**
Dalek Jast.

**DALEK CAAN**
Dalek Caan.

**THE DOCTOR**
So that's it! At last.. the Cult of Skaro. I thought you were just a legend.

**ROSE**
Who are they?

**THE DOCTOR**
A secret order. Above and beyond the Emperor himself. Their job was to imagine. Think as the enemy thinks. Even dared to have names.. All to find new ways of killing.

**DOOMSDAY**
by Russell T Davies

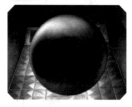

## The Void Ship

A Void Ship is a theoretical impossibility: a craft designed to exist outside space and time and travel through the Void – an area of absolute nothing between parallel universes. Somehow, the Cult of Skaro constructed a Void Ship during the closing stages of the Time War and escaped into the Void with the Genesis Ark.

The Dalek Void Ship re-emerged into this reality via an anomaly 240 metres above sea level in London's Docklands area. Naming it 'the Sphere', the Torchwood Institute contained it in a specially constructed 'Sphere Room' and attempted to examine it. It defied analysis: it weighed nothing, had no quantifiable age, emitted neither heat nor radiation, and had no atomic mass. By all normal measures, the Sphere did not exist.

# The Genesis Ark

A stolen Time Lord prison ship, it was not much larger than a Dalek on the outside, but it was bigger on the inside and contained millions of Daleks. The Cult of Skaro could not open it, however, as it could only be activated by the touch of an organic time traveller. Once it was triggered by Mickey Smith, the Cult took it to an open area and released the Dalek army into London's skies.

# The Cybermen

The Cybermen were created on a parallel Earth by the crippled inventor and businessman John Lumic. Designated 'Human.2', they were robotic casings which held reprogrammed human brains, prevented from feeling any pain by an emotional inhibitor.

Once the Cult's Void Ship had created the breach in the barrier between parallel dimensions, the Cybermen followed it through and invaded Earth. When the Daleks emerged, the Cybermen viewed an alliance between the two races as logical. The offer was rejected, and the two forces went into battle at Canary Wharf.

The Cybermen were sucked back into the Void, where they managed to steal a complete database on the Doctor from the Daleks, along with a device called a Dimension Vault. When the walls between parallel worlds weakened again, the Cybermen slipped out of the Void, falling through dimensions, and used the Dimension Vault to travel back in time to Victorian London.

# Elevate!

Geocomtex facility, Utah, 2012

Earth, 200,100

The Torchwood Institute, London, 2007

Hooverville, New York, 1930

The Crucible in the Medusa Cascade

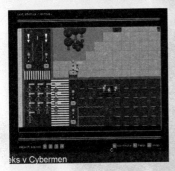

ks v Cybermen

## Daleks vs. Cybermen

After the huge success of *The Last Dalek* in 2005, the BBC's official *Doctor Who* website featured a new game for every episode of Series Two in 2006. This culminated with *Daleks vs. Cybermen* on 8 July, after *Doomsday*'s broadcast. Based on the Battle of Canary Wharf, it was a strategy game that challenged the player to prevent a Dalek invasion by carefully arranging Cyberman forces. It was designed by the Welsh games firm Sequence.

Many more games followed in subsequent years, including *Dalek Break-out* ('help a Dalek to avoid an explosive fate') and *Eye of the TARDIS*, in which the Doctor has become trapped in the TARDIS's memory core and players must help him get past avatars of his deadliest enemies to reach the data/matter converter and escape.

## Short Stories

Author Justin Richards wrote short stories for both *The Daleks* and *The Cult of Skaro*, two entries in the *Doctor Who Files* series from BBC Children's Books.

'Mission to Galacton' harked back to the *TVC21* adventures, showing a Dalek saucer despatched to Galacton to overcome the local population and harvest its mineral wealth, taking control of the planet's core.

'Birth of a Legend' explained the origins of the Cult of Skaro, introducing Dalek Sec as a Dalek Commander of a group responsible for destroying the Mechonoids. On the successful completion of this mission, the four Daleks are summoned by the Dalek Emperor, who informs them that they are to become the Cult of Skaro. He assigns them names and explains their mission to become the Daleks' greatest weapon. The story leaves them as they enter their new and secret Strategy Chambers on Skaro.

# WE'LL TAKE MANHATTAN

Only the Cult of Skaro escaped being dragged back into the Void, using all their resources to initiate an emergency temporal shift. The last four Daleks in existence found themselves stranded in 1930s New York,

📺 **DALEKS IN MANHATTAN / EVOLUTION OF THE DALEKS**
by Helen Raynor
Starring David Tennant as the Doctor
**First broadcast:** 21/04/2007– 28/04/2007

their power cells drained, on the brink of extinction. They established a concealed base under the Empire State building and constructed a vast genetics laboratory, with storage bays extending beneath Manhattan.

Initially, they attempted to breed new Dalek mutants with genetic material extracted from the members of the Cult. Their experiments were unsuccessful, inadequate power supplies preventing them from creating sustainable life.

The resulting lifeless genetic matter was discarded in the nearby sewers. The Cult then abducted scores of men from the city above, dividing their captives into two groups according to intelligence. Those of lower intellect were used as test subjects for experimental fusion of genetic elements, creating hybrids of pigs and human beings; the Daleks used these Pig Slaves to collect further human specimens. The more intelligent groups of captives were kept in suspended animation, a thousand bodies held near death and their minds wiped clean, ready for new input.

The Cult of Skaro now moved on to the Final Experiment. In the first phase, Dalek Sec absorbed and merged with a human subject to create the first Human-Dalek hybrid. In the second phase, the Cult intended to infuse the stored empty human shells with Dalek DNA to create a new race – a mobile army of Dalek-Human hybrids, freed from protective casings yet loyal to the Daleks. The children of Skaro would, finally, walk again. The plan required enormous reserves of power, which the Daleks would access by harnessing the energy from a blast of gamma radiation. They would use the antenna at the top of the Empire State as an energy conductor for radiation-carrying lightning, transmitting the power down through the building to the Dalek systems below, splicing Dalek DNA with the stored humans.

The Dalek Sec human hybrid, however, absorbed more than he expected – he gained aspects of humanity that the Daleks discounted as irrelevant. As he began to experience emotions and feel compassion, Sec concluded that the Dalek plan was flawed: the Daleks could benefit more from regaining the lost emotions they regarded as a weakness. He and the Doctor began to revise the Final Experiment so that a new race of Daleks could start again, but the rest of the Cult rejected Sec's analysis. They turned on him, and the original plan to create a Dalek-Human army was reinstated. The Doctor managed to introduce Time Lord DNA into the mix, giving the newly activated Dalek-Humans a measure of independence and free will, which caused them to question their orders. The Cult promptly designated the Experiment a failure and eliminated the race they had just created, though not before Daleks Sec, Jast and Thay had also been exterminated.

Of the whole Dalek race, only Dalek Caan now remained. He activated a last desperate emergency temporal shift to escape New York, then travelled across his own timeline and back into the Time War itself. It cost him his sanity, but Caan managed to penetrate the timelocked War, somehow reaching its earliest days and rescuing the Daleks' creator...

**TRACKING DALEK TIMELINES**

200,100 ➤➤ Dalek Emperor destroyed by the Bad Wolf ➤➤ 200,100
2007 ➤➤ The Battle of Canary Wharf ➤➤ 2007
1930 ➤➤ The Final Experiment in Manhattan ➤➤ 1930

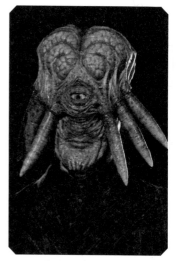

## Dalek Sec

Commander of the Seventh Dalek Incursion Squad until the Dalek Emperor named him and made him leader of the Cult of Skaro, Dalek Sec was distinguished by his black casing and was the most intelligent Dalek in their history. It was his plan, on reaching New York, to create a Dalek-Human army, knowing that the Dalek race could no longer survive if it did not evolve. The feelings of compassion and pity he suddenly felt after becoming the first Human-Dalek hybrid led the other Cult members to usurp him. He ended up in chains, watching as the other Daleks undid his plans to give the Daleks a new beginning, and finally sacrificed himself to save the Doctor.

## New Dalek Embryos

In the sewers beneath Manhattan, the Doctor discovered a piece of composite organic matter with a faint green glow and an unpleasant odour. Realising that it had been genetically engineered, he scanned it for a chromosomal reading and identified

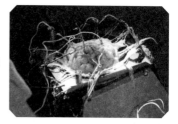

its fundamental DNA type as 467-989. That meant its planet of origin was Skaro.

Once they had set up their underground base, the Cult of Skaro had attempted to grow Dalek embryos. The artificial flesh they managed to create was too weak to survive, and the embryos were discarded – dumped in the Manhattan sewers.

## Pig Slaves

The failure of the embryos made the Cult of Skaro realise that the Daleks' only hope lay in harnessing Earth's primary resource: its human population.

Initial experiments were in splicing the DNA of different species – pigs and humans. The resultant hybrid was useful as a slave force, being both obedient and vicious, and they were used to snatch more victims from the streets above. The Pig Slaves had limited intelligence, though, and rapidly decayed, giving them a severely shortened lifespan.

One subject escaped before the hybridisation process finished. Though part converted, Laszlo retained his intelligence and free will. Even uncompleted, the process was irreversible, but the Doctor was able to arrest his physical decay.

## FILMING THE 'ENEMY'

Keen to preserve the mystery of what precisely viewers have to look forward to, the *Doctor Who* production team always ensure limited distribution of forthcoming scripts – the smallest possible number of cast and crew receive scripts, and it's not uncommon for the final few pages of some episodes to be withheld from all but the principal cast. Returning characters and monsters will sometimes be given an alternative name in the scripts – for *Evolution of the Daleks*, before its title was settled, the Cult of Skaro were referred to as 'Enemies 1, 2, 3 and 4' to avoid giving their identity away to extras and onlookers. During location shooting for the Hooverville scenes, everyone had a script saying 'Enemy', the flying Daleks

were to be added in post-production, the Dalek lines were read in without enhancement, and the word 'Dalek' was only used once. All was going to plan, until the crowd-scene extras were told: 'For your sightline, can you look up in the sky at this, please?' as a cardboard Dalek on a stick was held aloft for all to see...

## You Would Make a Good Dalek

Despite their innate contempt for all other life forms and total lack of mercy and pity, the Daleks have always possessed a keen insight into how these 'weaknesses' can be exploited in their opponents. They appreciate that most humanoid races have a need for trust, comfort, security, reassurance, and they are quite prepared to adopt and adapt the tactics of lesser species to advance their own cause.

Often, this is a simple analysis of the likely needs and desires of a lesser race, and of how those 'weaknesses' can be taken advantage of. The Thals needed assistance because their crops had failed, therefore the promise of food and water would lure them into an ambush. The rebels of 22nd-century London feared death, so they were offered life, in exchange for surrender and work.

During their earliest encounters, the Daleks exerted pressure on the Doctor by endangering the things they associated with him – the Emperor believed he could compel the Doctor to distribute the Dalek Factor by threatening to destroy the TARDIS, and a Dalek taskforce ransomed the lives of the Doctor's friends for the return of the taranium core.

Over time, the Daleks became aware that the Doctor holds all life sacrosanct – beginning the extermination of a small group of slave workers on Skaro was enough to force him to release Davros to them. The Dalek Emperor was certain that the Doctor would not unleash a lethal Delta Wave from the Game Station, knowing that it would kill not just the Daleks but all life on Earth too; he even risked taunting the Doctor for his 'cowardice'.

The lone Dalek encountered in Utah showed a high level of the same cunning – it was able to dupe Rose Tyler into touching it only because it understood how to manipulate her instinctive compassion, playing on her sympathy for its apparent loneliness, isolation and fear. Until its absorption of Rose's DNA began to take effect, it played a slow, deliberate game of undermining the Doctor's sense of self, constantly drawing parallels between the Time Lord and itself. When the Doctor confirmed the Dalek was alone in the universe, the creature waited just long enough for the last Time Lord to make the comparison himself before stating, 'We are the same,' knowing that this would goad the Doctor into a physical attack on it, hoping that the Doctor would touch its casing. It ensured the Doctor could watch its rampage through Van Statten's base, again provoking him into demanding its death – his anger and hatred making him, as it pointed out again, good Dalek material. When the Dalek took Rose hostage, asking the Doctor what purpose emotion had if it wasn't enough to make him save 'the woman he loved', the Doctor released it from the lower levels. But this was also enough to make the Doctor take up arms against it.

Clearly, Daleks are able to think as the enemy thinks in order to weaken them, but the Cult of Skaro were charged with taking this to extremes. Perhaps in order to avoid a repeat of the Movellan stalemate, these were Daleks ordered to think in an un-Dalek way, to contemplate such heresies as tampering with the purity of the Dalek race in order to ensure its survival in the Time War. This was the ultimate Dalek taboo – when the Emperor Dalek had made 'pure, blessed Daleks' by sifting human DNA, the resulting creatures hated themselves. When Dalek Sec concluded that the Children of Skaro must evolve a life outside the shell and walk again, it ultimately proved a step too far for the Cult of Skaro:

> **DALEK SEC**
> The Cult of Skaro was created by the Emperor for this very purpose. To imagine new ways of survival.
>
> **DALEK THAY**
> But we must remain pure.
>
> **DALEK SEC**
> No, Dalek Thay! Our purity has brought us to extinction! We must adapt to survive. You have all made sacrifices..
>
> **DALEKS IN MANHATTAN**
> by Helen Raynor

# THE NEW DALEK EMPIRE

📺 **THE STOLEN EARTH/ JOURNEY'S END** **by Russell T Davies** Starring David Tennant as the Doctor **First broadcast:** 28/06/2008– 05/07/2008

Having been rescued from the Time War, Davros once more began to build a new race of Daleks. This time, though, there was no species, human or Kaled, to scavenge from; Davros extracted cells from his own body from which he could extrapolate a whole new Dalek DNA and grow new mutations to inhabit and control his armoured travel machines. Unlike the earlier attempt by the Cult of Skaro, Davros the master scientist was successful. Each Dalek was imbued with the memories and knowledge that only Davros and Caan now shared, and each Dalek was born with the inevitable conviction of its own superiority over every other race in the cosmos. History quickly repeated itself – a new Supreme Dalek emerged to direct Dalek activities. Davros was kept alive, useful but merely tolerated, and held with Dalek Caan in the Crucible Vaults.

Millennia earlier in the Dalek timeline, Davros had pledged: 'I will arm the Daleks with new weaponry. Weaponry so devastating that all matter will succumb to its power.' Now, from his confinement, he devised that weapon and gave it to his new Dalek race. The Daleks had always been motivated by a hatred of all non-Dalek life. At last they could pursue that hatred to its logical end.

## The Reality Bomb

Twenty-seven planetary bodies were removed from time and space and assembled, like the pieces of an engine, in the Medusa Cascade to form a vast array, one second out of sync with the rest of the universe. The planetary array was held in perfect balance in an optimum moving pattern of slow orbits. At the centre of the Medusa Cascade was the spherical command ship, the Crucible, at the heart of which was a core of Z-Neutrino Energy. As the Crucible reached 100 per cent efficiency, the planetary alignment field was activated – the planets' configuration flattened the Z-Neutrino Energy into a single string, and the array formed a transmitter to send the compressed Energy across the universes. This was the Reality Bomb, and its detonation would separate every form of matter into its constituent particles by cancelling out the electrical field that binds atoms together. Those particles would crumble to dust, which would dissolve into nothing in a chilling echo of the Time Lords' own plan to bring the Time War to an end. Breaking through the Medusa Cascade's rift into every dimension and parallel, on full transmission the Bomb would destroy reality itself.

**TRACKING DALEK TIMELINES**
2007 >> The Battle of Canary Wharf >> 2007
1930 >> The Final Experiment in Manhattan >> 1930
**2009 >> Earth removed to the Medusa Cascade >> 2009**

Earth and the other stolen worlds all suffered the same fate: without warning, they were lifted out of their orbits and transported across space and time. The inhabitants experienced what seemed to be massive earthquakes as their planets were stolen, before discovering that the skies above were now filled with other worlds.

## RECREATING DAVROS

Actor Julian Bleach took the role of Davros in 2008, following an appearance in *Torchwood* as the Ghost Maker. A new mask was made by Millennium FX and a chair built by the *Doctor Who* Art Department. Both were updated, but closely followed the original 1975 designs.

Then the new Dalek fleet descended, hundreds of thousands of Daleks making planetfall and beginning to harvest the population. All resistance was eliminated: strategic and military points were destroyed or disabled and key political figures exterminated; buildings were set ablaze, and prisoners were rounded up and transported to the Crucible as test subjects for the Reality Bomb.

A number of the Doctor's friends and former travelling companions united to guide him to the relocated Earth, from where he boarded the Crucible to confront Davros and the Supreme Dalek. With Rose Tyler, he was taken prisoner and held in the Crucible's lower-level Vaults, a plaything for Davros. But a unique space-time event occurred on board the TARDIS: a two-way biological metacrisis created a part-human duplicate Doctor and a part-Time Lord Donna Noble. They entered Davros's Vault where Donna deactivated the Reality Bomb, while disabling all Dalek weapons and scrambling their control circuits. The Doctor, his duplicate and Donna then returned all the stolen planets to their points of origin.

To the Doctor's anger, the duplicate Doctor then maximised the Dalekenium power feeds and blasted them back into the Crucible. All Dalek forces in the Medusa Cascade were entirely wiped out in an apparent genocide.

## Dalek Caan

The last remaining Dalek in all of time and space after the destruction of the rest of the Cult of Skaro, Dalek Caan's impossible journey into the Time War to save Davros drove him insane. His casing was all but destroyed in the process, leaving the mutant creature within exposed and hanging out of its shattered shell. His mind became twisted, attuned to the fluctuating possibilities of the timelines – raving in his casing, he became a prophet,

able to foretell and, to some extent, shape the future. And now he knew that he did not actually want his race to survive. He manipulated events to help bring the Doctor and his companions to the Crucible, knowing that it could mean a final end for the Daleks at last.

## The Supreme Dalek

The Supreme Dalek was the first of the new race of Daleks created by Davros from his own genetic material after escaping from the Time War. It was red, significantly larger than those of the other Daleks, with gold hemispheres on its lower casing, a third light to the rear of its dome and large golden clamps fitted to its front and sides.

## VOICING AN ICON

Actor Nicholas Briggs has 'an infinite number of Dalek voices to do – a vast library of them in my head', but the insane Dalek Caan wasn't one of them. It was one of the most challenging, but also 'an utter joy. Once I'd cottoned on to the idea that he was in a constant state of insane joy, I nailed it. So much of it was described so well in Russell's script, but director Graeme Harper was brilliant and kept telling me, "I love the laughing!"'

# DESIGNING THE NEW DALEK EMPIRE

Conceptual artwork for *The Stolen Earth* and *Journey's End* by designer Peter McKinstry

# Interfering in History

Daleks do not care about history.

When the Time Lords broke their own rules and sent the Doctor back to the Daleks' creation, Davros promptly sought to gain foreknowledge of, and so prevent, every future Dalek defeat. This typifies the Daleks approach to time travel – when the Doctor foiled their invasion of Earth, they first tried to wipe him out of history, then later reinvaded the planet at an earlier point in time to try and avert their defeat.

The Daleks have been present on many previous occasions in Earth's past:

**》》c.2650 BC:** The Daleks battle with Egyptian soldiers during the construction of the Great Pyramids

**》》AD 102:** The Daleks lead an alien alliance to Stonehenge to capture the Doctor

**》》25 November 1872:** The Daleks land on the Mary Celeste, causing the crew to abandon ship

**》》1866:** The Daleks bring time-corridor technology to Theodore Maxtible's house in Victorian England; the house is destroyed on 3 June

**》》1930:** The Cult of Skaro establishes a base beneath the Empire State Building and begins kidnapping locals to build armies of Pig Slaves and Dalek-Humans; on 1 November, a lightning strike supplies gamma radiation to activate the Dalek-Human force

**》》1941:** In the guise of 'Ironsides', the Daleks join Churchill's war effort while awaiting the arrival of the Doctor; they are used to repel an air raid, destroying several German bombers

**》》c.1960:** A lone Dalek falls through time to Ascension Island

**》》November 1963:** Two Dalek factions fight for the Hand of Omega in Shoreditch, London, killing a number of British soldiers

**》》1966:** A Dalek timeship lands in the Empire State Building, New York

**》》1966:** The Daleks help Edward Waterfield travel from 1866 via a time corridor; he establishes a successful antiques business. On 20 July, a Dalek uses the time corridor to travel from 1866 to monitor the capture of the Doctor; it exterminates a man called Kennedy

**1970s:** A Dalek and Ogron taskforce attacks Auderley House ahead of a peace conference; the house is destroyed in an explosion, but the peace delegates survive

**1984:** The Daleks establish a time-corridor opening in East London, duplicating members of the British Army and storing Movellan virus samples in a disused warehouse

**1996:** A Dalek squad lands in Frankenstein's House of Horror at the Festival of Ghana

**1996:** A stone Dalek is restored to life by the Pandorica and rampages through the National Museum in pursuit of the Doctor

**2007:** Millions of Daleks take to the skies above Canary Wharf, battling the Cybermen and exterminating humans

**2009:** The Earth is removed from its solar system and transported to the Medusa Cascade to become a component in the Reality Bomb

# A FIXED POINT

The new Dalek invasion of Earth of 2009 spared one particular human. Ten-year-old Adelaide Brooke watched as a Dalek hovered outside her house, its eyestalk scanning

her, then flew away. The death of Adelaide Brooke on 21 November 2059 is a fixed point in time, and the Dalek must have identified her younger self. Even for Daleks, it seems, there are some events that cannot be altered.

📺 **THE WATERS OF MARS**
by Russell T Davies and Phil Ford
Starring David Tennant as the Doctor
**First broadcast:** 15/11/2009

# The Attachment Detachment

Magnetised manipulator arm capable of holding metal sheet

Blowtorch attachment, able to burn through metal doors and walls

Seismic detector/perceptor, able to pinpoint spatial location of TARDIS

Electrode unit, used to override door controls in Mechonoid city

Pyroflame attachment, used for defoliation of jungle planets

Scoop attachment, used to dispense Dalek mutants into casings

Welding tool attachment, used in Spiridon city

Sucker attachment used to calculate combination locks

 Sucker attachment used to crush human skull

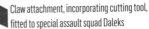 Claw attachment, incorporating cutting tool, fitted to special assault squad Daleks

Sucker attachment used to scan and assess or extract and assimilate brainwaves

Syringe attachment used to inject chromatin solution

Special attachment on Vault Daleks aboard Crucible for technical operations

# DALEKMANIA

## Extermination of the Daleks

*Doctor Who: Battles in Time* was a fortnightly magazine and trading-card collection for children. Published from 2006 to 2009, it included a regular comic strip. From 12 November to 24 December 2008, there was a brand new Dalek adventure in four parts: *Carnage Zoo*, *Flight and Fury*, *The Living Ghosts* and *Extermination of the Daleks*.

Travelling alone after *Journey's End*, the Doctor uncovers a Dalek disguised as a cleaning robot in a zoo. The Dalek makes off with a caged Krikoosh, a creature made of unstable molecules that can pass through solid objects. The Doctor pursues them and rescues the Krikoosh, but realises that the Dalek was actually seeking the shielding of the creature's cage – the Daleks need its protection from their own new intangibility weapon, with which they turn all humans into ghosts.

The strip was written by Steve Cole with art by Lee Sullivan.

## How to Draw a Dalek by Lee Sullivan

Lee Sullivan has drawn Dalek comic strips extensively for *Doctor Who Magazine*, *Doctor Who Adventures* and *Doctor Who: Battles in Time*. Here's his guide to how to do it – coming soon to a pencil case near you:

'Daleks have always been lovely things to draw because they are such a precise set of shapes and angles. I've always liked looking at the relationships between the discs, hemispheres and the subtle angles of the flat surfaces.

'It's interesting that the early (great) work in *The Dalek Book* and *TVC21* by Ron Jennings and Ron Turner shows the Daleks in a much more simplified form – presumably because the reference they were working to was scant. They are depicted as more of a rounded cone, but the genius thing about the original design is how it turns from a dome and flared cylindrical top half into a much sharper, angular skirt section. The hemis (as we Dalek nuts call the balls on the skirt section) unify the design and echo the arm articulation and sucker. That's what I always try to show in my strips – the strange beauty of the Dalek; the movement of the head (like a turret on a tank) and the eyestalk; the exact proportions. They are much easier to draw from below, as the flared shape is somewhat lost when you look down on them.

'The 2005 Daleks are far more complex from a detail point of view, but were the same basic shape, whereas the latest versions have moved away from the classic Dalek shape, proportions and size.'

## Prisoner of the Daleks

BBC Books' *Doctor Who* novels range continued through the Ninth Doctor's tenure and on into the Tenth's, but it was not until April 2009 that the Daleks made another appearance.

Trevor Baxendale's novel pits the Doctor against a particularly cruel Dalek – Dalek X, their Inquisitor General. Dalek X's black casing with gold globes is based on a Dalek design seen not on TV but in toyshops – as part of the Radio Controlled Dalek Battle Pack first released in late 2005.

*Prisoner of the Daleks* incorporates various classic Dalek scenarios, culminating in a slave mine at the heart of a planet's core. The Daleks intend to use a Large Chronon Collider to access the Time Vortex and use its power to defeat the Time Lords. The novel also explains, for the first time, exactly how a Dalek's weapon works:

'... You know how those Dalek guns work, don't you? On full power, they can blast a human being into atoms in a split second. But they never do that. Every Dalek dials down the power on its gun-stick to the specific level that will kill a human being. Then they lower the power setting just a tiny bit further, so that the beam burns away the central nervous system from the outside in, meaning that every human being dies in agony. So it takes a full two to three seconds for a Dalek to exterminate one of us – and that's deliberate.'

## The Second Coming

Since 2005, the Daleks have taken their rightful place as the supreme beings... of the UK's shops. They adorn everything from slippers, pyjamas, T-shirts, socks and underwear to pencil cases and lunchboxes, cakes and Easter eggs. There have been Dalek action figures, remote-controlled Daleks, talking Daleks, even a huge voice-controlled Dalek. The Cult of Skaro came with their very own Genesis Ark. The Radio Controlled Dalek Battle Pack pitched a couple of Daleks against

each other. The Voice Changer Helmets allowed kids to become a standard Dalek, Dalek Sec or even the Dalek Sec Human Hybrid. The Daleks have once again conquered the toyshops.

## Purity

> Inside that shell is a creature born to hate, whose only thought is to destroy everything and everyone that isn't a Dalek too. It won't stop until it's killed every human being alive.

The Doctor once described the Daleks as 'only half-robot ... Inside each of those shells is a living, bubbling lump of hate.' Their ultimate goal is a universe that contains only Dalek life. Anything else is anathema to them. They are the ultimate example of a dislike for the unlike.

The wider their world view, the grander their desire. When they believed themselves alone in their city, they were the closest the Daleks have ever been to content. Their instant response to the return of the Thals was to strive to restore the status quo by exploding a neutron bomb. Learning of life on other worlds changed this irrevocably: the Daleks became determined to seek, locate and annihilate it all. Genetically programmed to believe themselves the supreme beings, the Daleks have even breached the Void between the universes in order to destroy all possible life in all possible realities, such is their determination to be the only viable life form. This is not even limited to organic matter, as their vendettas against the robotic Mechonoids and Movellans show. It is not even sufficient to be physically Dalek – even Daleks who think differently are regarded as impure, as the Civil War demonstrated. The ultimate Dalek goal is to be the sole creature in existence, to return to the state they were in before the Doctor first arrived on Skaro.

Yet their programming also tells them that their race must endure, and so the Daleks have adapted constantly to achieve this. They were prepared to add characteristics from other species – the Spiridons' invisibility, say – to strengthen their forces. They wanted Davros to reprogram them to break the Movellan stalemate. Davros used human beings to begin a new Dalek army, and the mutants he installed in his Imperial Daleks were quite different to the underdeveloped originals. They mutated further during the Time War, and the Cult of Skaro created Dalek-Human hybrids. They spent centuries mixing their genes with other races simply to survive – the Dalek Emperor filtered human flesh for new Dalek material, and Davros sampled his own cells to create more Daleks.

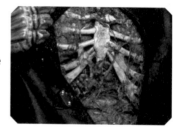

So would one of the very earliest Daleks even recognise a Dalek from beyond the Time War...?

# THE NEW DALEK PARADIGM

VICTORY OF
THE DALEKS
by Mark Gatiss
Starring Matt Smith
as the Doctor
First broadcast:
17/04/2010

A single Dalek ship survived the carnage of the Medusa Cascade. Crippled and dying, it fell back through time to Earth's solar system in the first half of the 20th century, where its crew located a long-lost Progenitor device. These Daleks, though, were unable to activate the device: their genetic inheritance was now so muddled and distorted from its Kaled roots that the Progenitor would not recognise them as pure Daleks. The key to that recognition, ironically, lay with the Doctor, who by now formed so fundamental a part of Dalek history that their own device would accept his testimony over theirs. The remaining Daleks therefore devised a plan to attract the Doctor's attention and cause him to identify them as Daleks.

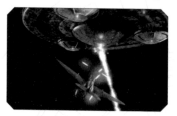

In 1941, Earth's Second World War was at its height. The Daleks covertly supplied the British with data and theories to produce advanced weapons that could end the war. Foremost of these was a 'new' robotic force – the Ironsides – and Great Britain's Prime Minister, Winston Churchill, ordered their rapid deployment against the Nazi forces.

Enthusiastic as he was about his new secret weapon, however, Churchill was cautious enough to request advice from an old friend – the Doctor. He summoned the TARDIS to London, where the Doctor was appalled to discover a small force of khaki-coloured Daleks apparently following British orders and acting as obedient servants and loyal troops. He insisted that these so-called Ironsides were a danger, telling Churchill that his new soldiers were in fact Daleks. The Doctor's word was enough to activate the recovered Progenitor, and within minutes a new officer class of pure Daleks was created.

This New Dalek Paradigm immediately assumed control of the remaining Dalek saucer, cleansing their race of the last of the impure Daleks. They forced the Doctor to call off an attack on their ship by Spitfire fighter planes protected by gravity bubbles, then activated a time corridor and time-jumped out of the solar system. Back to their own time to begin to rebuild...

# Edwin Bracewell

Professor Bracewell was a Dalek duplicate with no idea that he was in fact a robot powered by an Oblivion Continuum capable of destroying the world. He genuinely believed that the Ironsides were his invention, along with bubbles of artificial gravity and a portable television that could pick up transmissions from an orbiting Dalek spacecraft.

# The Ironsides

Churchill's secret weapons proved themselves with deadly accuracy as they shot down Luftwaffe aircraft from Whitehall's roofs, and they promised even greater success when they became offensive rather than defensive weapons. The British Government had even prepared propaganda material promoting the Ironsides' key role in the forthcoming victory over Nazi Germany.

The Ironsides proved themselves more than just obedient soldiers – they were also present in the War Rooms beneath Whitehall, where they performed menial tasks and proved adept at carrying trays of tea, repeatedly asserting that they were dutiful soldiers and servants, dedicated only to winning the war.

# The Progenitor Device

Millennia earlier, the Daleks had created thousands of race banks that were scattered through time and space as insurance against possible Dalek defeats. The Daleks stranded on Vulcan had something similar aboard their timeship – if activated by surviving Daleks, it contained enough pure genetic material to extrapolate a new paradigm and build a new race of Daleks. The locations of the Progenitor devices were all lost, and the surviving Daleks regarded them as a myth, until they actually found one.

On activation, the egg-like Progenitor transmitted its genetic data to a specially prepared chamber aboard the Dalek spacecraft. From the outside, the chamber's contents seemed to boil and blaze, with a flare of brilliant red light behind an impenetrable bank of smoke. The process complete, the machine powered down and its glass front opened to reveal the restoration of the Daleks...

ENEMY 1
We have succeeded. Dalek victory is complete! The Progenitor has restored our original genetic code.

WHITE ENEMY
Yes.

Beat.

You are inferior.

ENEMY 1
Yes.

WHITE ENEMY
Then, prepare.

ENEMIES 1, 2 and 3 raise their exterminators into the air.

ENEMIES 1, 2, 3
All hail the new Daleks!
All hail the new Daleks!

WHITE ENEMY
Cleanse the unclean!
Total obliteration.
DISINTEGRATE!

**VICTORY OF THE DALEKS**
by Mark Gatiss

## VOICING THE PARADIGM

'The Dalek Supreme is by far the gruffest Dalek voice I've ever done,' says Nicholas Briggs. 'The director, Andrew Gunn, said he wanted that, so I went for it. I also changed the modulation quite drastically. It still sounds very Daleky, but it's changed quite a bit. For *Victory of the Daleks*, Brynn the sound man had to keep twirling the modulator dials between lines to change the voice for me. But for *The Pandorica Opens*, which also featured Cybermen, I used two ring modulators, preset to their respective Cyberman and Dalek effects. Much less hassle!'

# WRITING THE PARADIGM

Mark Gatiss, the writer of *Victory of the Daleks*, explains that the birth of a new race of Daleks was conceived as a way to get beyond the only Daleks in existence being those that had somehow survived the Time War. 'The Daleks couldn't go on being brought back, only to be wiped out again. Steven Moffat felt that the Time War had been dealt with, and it was time the Daleks were back as a constant in the Doctor's life. Also, because there was so much "new" in the series it felt like a good idea to renew the Daleks.'

Mark and Steven wanted the size and colour of the New Dalek Paradigm to mark a complete shift from the bronze Daleks. 'Right from the start, I was very keen that the Daleks reflected the 1960s movie ones. When I was a kid, they were such a dynamic and colourful presence, and I just adored them. I thought it'd be fun to make them quite a bit bigger (although that turned out to have practical implications) and very Technicolor, although originally they were going to be Gold, Silver, Red, Green and Blue (I think).'

Four of the five members of the Paradigm have clearly defined roles – Drone, Scientist, Strategist and Supreme. But what is the Eternal? 'The Eternal is an enigmatic Dalek, liveried in yellow and black (nature's danger colours),' says Mark. 'Its exact function is a total mystery, but it's probably something to do with the Progenitor device and the continuation of the race.'

The episode also presents an end for 'the only survivors from Davros's reality bomb plan' – the remaining bronze Daleks who disguise themselves as the servile Ironsides. '*The Power of the Daleks* is a favourite of mine, and I knew I wanted to have some fun with that idea of the Doctor being the only one who knows what the Daleks really are. Once I'd come up with the idea of someone passing them off as an Earth-bound war machine and that they were being devious (which is the Daleks' best quality, I think) it was natural that they would be able to say the sort of things they never ordinarily can! I was immediately tickled by the idea of a domesticated Dalek asking someone if they wanted tea. And the Doctor's mounting frustration as these horrible killers play by the rules of English etiquette!'

The Paradigm escape triumphant at the end of the story. What does Mark think happens next? 'The new Daleks use their time corridor to find a quiet corner of space to breed terrible things, and everyone's happy. Except the rest of the universe, which will be ruthlessly EXTERMINATED!'

## DALEKMANIA

### City of the Daleks

There weren't 13 episodes in Series Five, there were 17 – and 4 of them were interactive. *The Adventure Games* are four extra *Doctor Who* stories, downloadable from the official *Doctor Who* website, and giving players the chance to join in with the adventure. The games were developed by Sumo Digital, with Matt Smith and Karen recording the Doctor and Amy's dialogue, alongside Nicholas Briggs voicing the Daleks. The first game, released at the start of June 2010, was *City of the Daleks*.

Written by Phil Ford, the game opens with the Doctor and Amy exploring the ruins of Dalek-occupied London. 'I remember thinking how brilliant they looked rendered in 3D,' says script editor Gary Russell. 'There's something very striking about that bright, primary-coloured Dalek against the background of devastation and decay which the post-apocalyptic 1963 offered.' When the action moves to Skaro, the Doctor and Amy explore the New Dalek Paradigm's City – named Kalaann. 'Phil came up with that,' says Gary. 'We thought

it sounded very *TVC21*, which was the feel that Phil and I wanted.'

Among countless Dalek artefacts in Kalaann is the casing of the Dalek Emperor – who viewers saw destroyed in *The Parting of the Ways*... So where has that come from? How have the Daleks invaded 1960s London? And what's Skaro doing being resurrected again? 'The New Dalek Paradigm took the Eye of Time from the Time War and returned to the destroyed Kalaann to rebuild it,' explains Gary. 'Only for the Doctor to put time back on the right path at the end. But with what happens in *The Big Bang*, who knows how much of Dalek history has been rewritten, revised or reworked, both with the new Paradigm and the old bronze Time War Daleks...'

# DALEK PARADIGMS

## 1963–1965

▶▶ TV: The Daleks, The Space Museum ▶▶ Height: 152 cm ▶▶ Fibreglass casing painted silver with 56 (14 X 4) blue sensor globes ▶▶ Flashing dome lights synchronised with speech ▶▶ Eyestalk with six discs behind eyepiece with contracting iris ▶▶ Telescopic sucker arm (with electromagnet) and gunstick fitted to midsection ▶▶ See pp. 19–21

## 1964

▶▶ TV: The Dalek Invasion of Earth ▶▶ Radar-type dish fitted to rear of casing ▶▶ Enlarged fender at base of skirt, concealing three pneumatic tyres ▶▶ Skirt panels painted alternate black and silver (Saucer Commander) or black (Black Dalek)

## 1965–1967

▶▶ TV: The Chase, The Daleks' Master Plan, The Power of the Daleks, The Evil of the Daleks ▶▶ Vertical slats fitted to shoulder section ▶▶ Only dome painted black for Dalek Emperor's Black Daleks (The Evil of the Daleks)

## 1972–1985

▶▶ TV: Day of the Daleks, Frontier in Space, Planet of the Daleks, Death to the Daleks, Genesis of the Daleks, Destiny of the Daleks, The Five Doctors, Resurrection of the Daleks, Revelation of the Daleks ▶▶ Casing painted gun-metal grey with black globes ▶▶ Taskforce Commander painted gold ▶▶ Dalek Supreme adapted from movie Dalek, with enlarged fender, black and gold-painted casing with gold globes, larger dome lights and torch-like eyepiece (Planet of the Daleks)

## 1974–1984

▶▶ Light grey casing, projectile gunstick, amber dome lights for taskforce leader (Death to the Daleks). ▶▶ Grey /black casing (Destiny of the Daleks). ▶▶ Black/white casing for Supreme Dalek (Resurrection of the Daleks)

## 1985–1988

▶▶ TV: Revelation of the Daleks, Remembrance of the Daleks ▶▶ Imperial Daleks painted white/gold; Renegade Daleks black/grey; Supreme Dalek black/silver ▶▶ Narrower, less tapered casings

## 2005–2010

▶▶ TV: Dalek, Bad Wolf, The Parting of the Ways, Army of Ghosts, Doomsday, Daleks in Manhattan, Evolution of the Daleks, The Stolen Earth, Journey's End, The Waters of Mars, Victory of the Daleks ▶▶ Height: Height: 165 cm Width: 100 cm Depth: 132 cm ▶▶ Identity tag below eyestalk ▶▶ Black domes for Emperor's guard ▶▶ Black casing for Dalek Sec ▶▶ Supreme Dalek has larger, red-painted casing ▶▶ See pp.109–11, 134–5

## 2010

▶▶ TV: Victory of the Daleks, The Pandorica Opens, The Big Bang ▶▶ Ironsides painted khaki, with Union flag replacing identity tag below eyestalk ▶▶ New Dalek Paradigm Height: 190 cm Width: 102 cm Depth: 135cm ▶▶ See pp.152–5

# DESIGNING THE NEW DALEK PARADIGM

**ETERNAL**  **DRONE**  **SUPREME**  **SCIENTIST**  **STRATEGIST**

'The prospect of redesigning the Daleks came up quite early in the production of Series Five,' explains designer Peter McKinstry. 'It had been kept pretty quiet in the Art Department up until we actually got the script for *Victory of the Daleks*. There was an opportunity to really see what we could do to make them more imposing, without changing them too much and making them look totally un-Daleky.'

The design brief was 'bigger than we've ever seen them', but Peter trod carefully. 'As with any redesign of a *Doctor Who* icon, you have to look at the previous incarnations and update it in a way that makes it new and exciting but still related to what has gone before. Series Five was all

about the new look: new logo, new TARDIS, new sonic screwdriver, new companion, new Doctor. There was a feeling of everything changing, and the Daleks were part of that. It was clear the impact of having new Daleks as well as new everything else would be massive.'

You don't design new Daleks overnight. 'There was about a month spent on the redesign, submitting one version, getting feedback, tweaking it, and looking at the scale, to arrive at something that everyone was very enthusiastic and excited about. There were a few

variations along the way, some of which I think are being kept locked up for possible future use...'

One of the inspirations was the 1960s movie Dalek design. 'Mark Gatiss or Steven Moffat suggested they wanted to go back to something like that; not to copy, but they were held up as an example of how effective these big scaled-up Daleks could be. We went about as far as it's possible to go with the redesign – any further and it would have become unrecognisable as a Dalek. Overall the effect might look quite subtle to some (and more obvious to others) but in fact every part of the Dalek has been altered in some way.'

A question that Peter is asked a lot is why the Daleks suddenly got taller. 'The previous Daleks had ended up being eyestalk-to-eyeball with Billie Piper [Rose Tyler in Series One]. These new versions are eye-to-Dalek-eye with Matt Smith. We felt beefing them up and making them taller

RED                    BLUE        (TPRKS)

YELLOW [END]

NB
BLACK
GLOVES

ORANGE

WHITE        SUPREME      (TPRKS)

| DOCTOR WHO I | | TITLE DALEK COLOURS |
|---|---|---|
| DRAWN BY ART DEPT | | DATE AUG 8 |
| PRODUCER | DIRECTOR | DOP | PROPS MASTER |
| PROD DESIGNER | ASSOC DESIGNER | FABRICATION | CONSTRUCTION |
| SUP ART DIR | CHIEF SUP ART DIR | SFX | CGI |
| S/R ART DIR | SET DECORATOR | COSTUME | GRAPHICS |
| BBC CYMRU WALES 2006/2007 | | OTHER | |

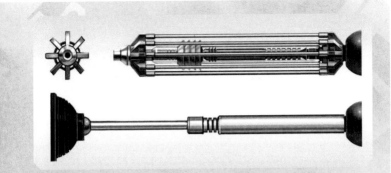

would revitalise the fear factor. I ended up broadening out the shoulder section, so that along with the added height, the new Daleks tower over the previous version and have a more muscular, more intimidating presence.'

There was one aspect of Peter's redesign that didn't make it through to the final build. 'I had hoped we would be able to carry the design through to its logical conclusion and actually give them a real metallic surface texture, preferably a stainless-steel finish, with brushed aluminium. The previous Daleks had been covered in rivets and bolts, whereas this new version was meant to be the opposite: you can't see where the pieces join, suggesting the casing is impenetrable. It's intended to be a sealed unit of alien design and technology.'

These are also the most colourful Daleks ever seen on screen. 'The new colours were mentioned in the script, but my concern was more for the overall look of them. The colours were eventually chosen, I think, after a lot of to-ing and fro-ing with Steven and the other executive producers.'

There were two other key changes. The new Daleks were designed with organic eyeballs. 'The actual fleshy eyeball idea came directly from Steven. It was at the part of the process when we were looking for something unique to this form of Dalek that set it apart. Eventually it was classed as too gruesome to transmit at 7pm on a Saturday night so it was altered slightly during the building process.' There's a reason for the other significant design change that has yet to be seen on screen: 'The spine section at the back provides an aperture that can open up and reveal new weapons.'

# THE PANDORICA

THE PANDORICA
OPENS / THE
BIG BANG
**by Steven Moffat**
Starring Matt Smith
as the Doctor
**First broadcast:**
19/06/2010–26/06/2010

In some unknown area of time and space, the New Dalek Paradigm began to rebuild the Dalek race. As they worked to assemble a vast new army, Dalek scientists monitored the galaxies in all eras. And then they discovered that the universe was on the point of complete obliteration – a final end that would not be brought about by the Daleks but would take the Daleks with it. There were cracks in the skin of the universe, in every time, ultimately emanating from the Doctor's TARDIS. It seemed that the Daleks' greatest foe would finally be the author of their destruction.

The new Dalek Supreme took the extraordinary decision to form a wide-ranging alien alliance of all those united by their fear and hatred of the Doctor. With their pooled resources and knowledge, the alliance lured the Doctor into a trap and imprisoned him in a specially constructed eternal prison – the Pandorica – reasoning that if he were separated from his time machine and incarcerated, he would be unable to complete the Total Event Collapse. So the mightiest military machine ever assembled surrounded Stonehenge in the Britain of AD 102, captured the Doctor and placed him inside the Pandorica for all eternity.

**TRACKING DALEK TIMELINES**
1941 ⟩⟩ The Ironside project ⟩⟩ 1941
102 ⟩⟩ The Pandorica alliance ⟩⟩ 102

It was not, however, the Doctor himself who was responsible for the end of the universe – it was the explosion of his TARDIS, an explosion he was unable to prevent because he was trapped inside the Pandorica. The TARDIS shattered, and all of creation was extinguished. As reality began to collapse, each member race of the alien alliance was deleted from history. Just the smallest traces remained – planet Earth would be the last flickering light to go out in the cosmos.

Of course, the Doctor did something astounding – he always does. Big Bang 2 restored the universe, rebooted it, with everything back in its proper place. The Daleks survived. (They always do, even when the Doctor loses everything.) Which means that out there, somewhere, at this moment in some far-flung future, the new Dalek Supreme is overseeing the building of the mightiest Dalek army ever assembled, plotting future victories and devising new ways to defeat the Doctor and destroy all non-Dalek life...

## The Alien Alliance

**CONFIRMED MEMBERS:** Daleks ▶▶ Cybermen ▶▶ Nestene Consciousness ▶▶ Sontarans ▶▶ Drahvins ▶▶ Homo Reptilia ▶▶ Draconians ▶▶ Zygons ▶▶ Terileptils ▶▶ Chelonians ▶▶ Slitheen ▶▶ Roboforms ▶▶ Sycorax ▶▶ Hoix ▶▶ Weevils ▶▶ Judoon ▶▶ Uvodni ▶▶ Atraxi ▶▶ Haemo-Goths

### Stone Daleks

1,894 years after the Doctor's imprisonment, the Pandorica was on display in Britain's National Museum, alongside the strange statues that had been found with it – the petrified remains of two Daleks, the last echoes of an erased existence. The reactivation of the Pandorica, however, also gave life to one of these stone Daleks. It pursued the now-freed Doctor and his friends through the Museum, attempting to exterminate the Doctor, and was eventually killed by River Song.

# DALEKMANIA

## The Only Good Dalek

In 2008, BBC Books' *Doctor Who* consultant Justin Richards proposed a new novel called 'The Dalek Project'. At the same time, he was also developing the first in a new range of graphic novels. 'Russell T Davies kept saying that the graphic novel needed to launch with something epic like "The Dalek Project",' Justin recalls, 'and eventually I took the hint... For various reasons, we didn't get to do "The Dalek Project" in 2009 and, with a new Doctor taking over, we felt we needed a different Dalek story. "The Dalek Project" is very much a Tenth Doctor story, so we put that aside – one day we'll do a Past Doctor graphic novel. Since "The Dalek Project" was set on Earth, I decided to do a huge space adventure for its replacement.'

*The Only Good Dalek*, published in September 2010, is set on Station 7, where Earth Forces send all the equipment captured during their unceasing war against the Daleks. 'It was nice to have an environment where I could legitimately play with all those past aspects of Dalek mythology,' says Justin. 'There's so much Dalek background stuff in the TV series that it's silly to invent more when you can do the same narrative things with Ogrons, Robomen and Varga plants. It was nice to be able to take what little we know about the Magneton, for instance, and use it as a plot point.' There's

also a couple of in-jokes about Dalek history: 'I loved the idea that the remote-control device should look just like the one you get with a real Dalek toy. And then, to identify the Daleks, because they all look pretty much the same, the humans put numbers on their domes – just like the production crew did in the first Dalek story. I liked the notion of them having the same solution to the problem.'

Justin and artist Mike Collins were also able to show off the New Dalek Paradigm. 'When I drafted the outline I didn't know the Dalek design was changing,' admits Justin. 'I originally wrote that the Daleks have had their solar-power slats removed so they have to draw energy from the floor. Then someone sent me a photo of the new Daleks and – no power slats! So I had to invent a power-inhibitor instead.'

## Doctor Who Live

With a script by Gareth Roberts, *Doctor Who* returned to the stage for a nationwide arena tour in October and November 2010, featuring a live band performing music from the series while the Great Vorgenson (Nigel Planer) exhibited his carnival of captured monsters, including Weeping Angels, Judoon and Sontarans. The show was part of an elaborate ruse to ensnare the Doctor (with specially shot footage of Matt Smith) – the Daleks had planted the idea in Vorgenson's mind. At the climax, the Daleks were defeated by upgraded Cybermen, and the new – levitating – Dalek Supreme was overcome by an audience-generated sonic wave.

## Handheld Daleks

November and December 2010 saw the Daleks appearing in three different games formats, featuring the voices of Matt Smith, Karen Gillan and Nicholas Briggs. Writer Oli Smith took a different approach for each one. '*Evacuation Earth* is a conversation-based point-and-click adventure for the Nintendo DS,' explains Oli, 'so we have lots of great speeches between the Doctor and the Daleks. The Daleks are rampaging through every level of the Wii game *Return to Earth*, and the iPhone game *The Mazes of Time* makes use of the different ranks of the New Dalek Paradigm. A Dalek Scientist acts as the catalyst for the adventure, when the Doctor helps botch one of his experiments. In gameplay terms, we used the Strategist as a more intimidating Dalek – they're smarter and harder to escape from than the Drones.'

Writing for the Daleks in game form has several challenges. 'I had to make them scary and intimidating in very few words. You have to be so brief and to-the-point with the Daleks, simply because they speak so slowly. Anything that approaches a chunky paragraph is too long for a game. Also curt Daleks work well when you're trying to reveal the plot through the player's actions rather than non-interactive speeches.'

Are the Daleks as lethal in game form? 'They shoot a lot more! It's harder to create that "stop and tell me all your plans" moment the Doctor needs because there has to be a reason for the Daleks not to shoot him after they've been blasting away for the last half-hour. I got around that by having them exterminate him anyway – but the Doctor has prepared for that eventuality...'

THIS IS ONLY THE BEGINNING. WE WILL PREPARE. WE WILL GROW STRONGER. WHEN THE TIME IS RIGHT, WE WILL EMERGE AND TAKE OUR RIGHTFUL PLACE AS THE SUPREME POWER OF THE UNIVERSE!

The Daleks were created to survive. Their city has been destroyed, their home planet obliterated, their entire race wiped from existence... and yet still the Daleks keep coming back.

The Daleks have conquered space, travelled beyond the universe, threatened every reality and challenged the most powerful race in the cosmos for control of Time itself. They cannot be reasoned with, they do not form genuine alliances, they do not want surrender. They will not rest until the only form of life in the universe is Dalek life. One day, the last word the last free creature in the universe will hear is...

# EXTERMINATE!